WHAT IS THIS PROFESSOR FREUD LIKE?

The History of Psychoanalysis Series

Professor Brett Kahr and Professor Peter L. Rudnytsky (Series Editors)

Other titles in the Series

WHAT IS THIS PROFESSOR FREUD LIKE?

A Diary of an Analysis with Historical Comments

Edited by

Anna Koellreuter

Translated by Kristina Pia Hofer

KARNAC

Originally published in Germany as »*Wie benimmt sich der Prof. Freud eigentlich?*«: *Ein neu entdecktes Tagebuch von 1921 historisch und analytisch kommentiert* edited by Anna Koellreuter

First published in English in 2016 by
Karnac Books Ltd
118 Finchley Road
London NW3 5HT

British Library Cataloguing in Publication Data

A C.I.P. for this book is available from the British Library

ISBN-13: 978-1-78220-414-5

Typeset by V Publishing Solutions Pvt Ltd., Chennai, India

www.karnacbooks.com

CONTENTS

ABOUT THE EDITOR AND CONTRIBUTORS

Editor

Anna Koellreuter, PhD, is a psychoanalyst and clinical psychologist in Zurich, and is a member of the Psychoanalytic Seminar in Zurich. Her publications are on the analysis of women by women, on the female analyst in the analytic process, and on the dynamics of drives in analysis. Her latest book is *Das Tabu des Begehrens. Zur Verflüchtigung des Sexuellen in Theorie und Praxis der feministischen Psychoanalyse* [The Taboo of Desire. On the Volatility of the Sexual in the Theory and Practice of Feminist Psychoanalysis] (Gießen: Psychosozial Verlag, 2001).

Contributors

Karl Fallend, PhD, is a professor of social psychology at August Aichhorn Institute, Graz, and an independent researcher based in Vienna. He has written extensively on the history of psychoanalysis, psychology and human rights, and National Socialism and its aftermath. Since 1984, he has been co-editor of *Werkblatt. Zeitschrift für Psychoanalyse und Gesellschaftskritik* [Werkblatt. Journal of Psychoanalysis and Social Criticism] (www.werkblatt.at).

Ernst Falzeder, PhD, is a senior research fellow at University College London, and works as an editor and translator for the Philemon Foundation, which makes available the complete works of C. G. Jung. He is a former research fellow at the universities of Geneva, Harvard, and Cornell Medical School. He was chief editor of the Freud-Ferenczi correspondence (Harvard), editor of the complete Freud-Abraham letters (Karnac), translator of Jung's seminar on children's dreams (Princeton), and editor, with John Beebe, as well as translator of Jung's correspondence with Hans Schmid-Guisan (Princeton). He has written more than two hundred publications on the history, theory, and technique of psychoanalysis and analytical psychology, the most recent being *Psychoanalytic Filiations: Mapping the Psychoanalytic Movement* (Karnac, 2015).

André E. Haynal, MD, is a psychoanalyst, a former president of the Swiss Psychoanalytic Society, and a recipient of the Sigourney Award for his life's work. He was the supervising editor of the Freud-Ferenczi correspondence, and has written twelve books, the most recent being *Disappearing and Reviving: Sándor Ferenczi in the History of Psychoanalysis* (Karnac, 2002).

SERIES EDITOR'S FOREWORD

Anna Koellreuter does not know that back in 2007 she cured me of a very frightening anxiety attack!

In the middle of a transatlantic crossing, the airplane on which I travelled encountered tremendous turbulence. The plane began to bump up and down, quite frighteningly—so much so that the cabin crew had to strap themselves into their seats. A number of passengers made increasingly audible noises, some crying out, "Oh, God … Oh, God!" As we jolted in our seats, I had to entertain the possibility that we might well crash.

Sitting alone in the back row, I decided that I could either subject myself to every nuance of the turbulence, or, I could reach into my carry-on luggage and choose something interesting to read in the hope of distracting myself. Happily, I had brought with me a copy of the newly published issue of the journal *Psychoanalysis and History*; and, intrigued to know that a psychoanalyst in Switzerland had just published a paper about her grandmother's analysis with Sigmund Freud, I began to read Dr Koellreuter's publication.

Within minutes, I found myself creatively transported to Vienna, 1921, and I proceeded to read with increasing interest Anna Koellreuter's account about how her grandmother, described in that article solely by the initial "G.", had travelled from Switzerland to undertake approximately four months of six-times weekly sessions—roughly eighty in all—with the father of psychoanalysis. Before long, the jerky movements of my British Airways flight no longer troubled me, and I became enraptured by Dr Anna Koellreuter's accomplished prose (rendered beautifully into English by Dr Ernst Falzeder), and by the privileged opportunity to hear Freud speak in such a vivid manner.

So, I owe Dr Koellreuter a huge debt of thanks for helping me to navigate a rather terrifying experience!

Not long after the publication of her journal article, Koellreuter produced a full-length book about her grandmother's diary, which appeared first in German (Koellreuter, 2009) and then in French (Anna G., 2010), each of which I read with fascination, never suspecting that only a few years' hence, we would have the opportunity to publish an English-language version of her wonderful contribution to psychoanalytical scholarship.

As historians will know only too well, many of Freud's former patients have written book-length memoirs about their experiences in analysis, which include the charming and engaging autobiography by the American psychoanalyst Dr Abram Kardiner (1977), *My Analysis with Freud: Reminiscences*, as well as the more sceptical tribute by the American psychiatrist Professor Joseph Wortis (1954), *Fragments of an Analysis with Freud*, and many others to boot (e.g., H.D. [Hilda Doolittle], 1956; Dorsey, 1976; Pohlen, 2006), not to mention the shorter accounts provided by Professor Paul Roazen (1995) in his book *How Freud Worked: First-Hand Accounts of Patients*. But in spite of the tremendous value afforded by these publications, many composed decades afterwards, few accounts have the immediacy of the diaries of Anna Koellreuter's grandmother, whose name can now be revealed in full as Dr Anna Guggenbühl.

Reading through Dr Guggenbühl's diary, one senses that, like many a dedicated analysand, she attended each of her sessions and then, afterwards, might have popped into a local *Kaffeehaus* in order to jot down some of her thoughts, her free associations, her dreams and, of most importance, Freud's words, in as much detail as she could remember. Thus, this extraordinary book grants us the rare opportunity to hear Freud speaking to a patient directly, offering us one of the best glimpses into how he actually talked, how he formulated interpretations, and how he worked in the transference.

Throughout the diary, we obtain a rich glimpse into the nature of psychoanalytical conversations in the early 1920s and into the range of techniques which Freud employed. Certainly, we know that Dr Guggenbühl spoke extensively about her dreams, and shared many intimate details with Freud; we also come to learn that both Freud and Guggenbühl discussed sexuality and bodily functions with great frankness, covering such topics as masturbation, genitalia, urine, faeces, and semen. One cannot quite imagine any other setting in which a young female physician could speak about these matters in such a direct fashion with a much older man.

In terms of technical interventions, Freud certainly privileged the interpretation, sharing both genetic interpretations about the meaning of past events in the patient's life, as well as transference interpretations, explaining her material in terms of the psychoanalytical relationship. But he also asked the patient direct questions; he analysed her dreams; he interpreted resistance; he forged links between sessions, cross-referencing material; he formulated constructions and reconstructions; he made clarificatory comments and provided explanations; and he offered didactic instruction in the symbolism of dreams, *inter alia*. One might assume that Freud also utilised silence—the very bedrock of clinical practice, both then and now—although in the diary, we cannot, of course, hear Freud's silences as palpably as his words. Thus, we form a picture of Freud as an accomplished conversationalist who covered a broad range of topics in a wide variety of styles, eliciting compelling free associative material, dream material, sexual material, and early memories, in a fluid fashion.

Above all, we have the opportunity to observe Freud making "classical" connections, interpreting lovers in adult life as reincarnations of the patient's father and brothers. Clearly, the interpretation of oedipal material takes pride of place.

Modern readers of this nearly century-old diary may enjoy the experience of watching Freud making a host of astute interconnections, but from the comforts of our chairs nearly one hundred years later, we can, from time to time, assume the role of posthumous supervisor, and wonder whether Freud missed out on the meaning of certain pieces of the patient's material. For instance, in extract 20, Dr Guggenbühl made a reference to "an elderly gentleman", of whom she wrote, "it was as if he knew about everything". Although referring, ostensibly, to a man acquainted with her boyfriend, one wonders whether this remark might represent a piece of transference to Freud, the elderly, omniscient man, who understands it all. Indeed, this diary entry precedes the patient's declaration of love for Freud's genius not long thereafter. Perhaps Freud did make such a transference interpretation, although the diary does not provide evidence one way or the other.

Anna Guggenbühl's text has also furnished us with other snippets of fascinating information. For instance, we encounter a reference to "Leporello", the character from Wolfgang Amadeus Mozart's opera *Don Giovanni*, provided by the ostensibly non-musical Freud. Additionally, we learn that Freud did not have an entirely soundproof office; and in extract 35, dated 26th April, 1921, Guggenbühl reported that while sitting in Freud's waiting-room at the Berggasse, she could hear a patient, then in session, talking about chorophyll! It would be hugely tempting to identity this chorophyll-speaking patient as Arthur Tansley, the English botanist; but it seems that he did not begin his analysis with Freud until some months after Guggenbühl had completed her own treatment (e.g., Cameron and Forrester, 1999, 2000).

Above all, we learn yet again how closely Freud paid attention to his patient's discourse, relishing the detail of Dr Guggenbühl's communications. Thus, the precancerous Freud who emerges from this diary might be described as a very alert, very awake, and very alive Sigmund Freud. Indeed, sharing yet another family memory, the editor and granddaughter Anna Koellreuter has written: "My mother remembers a remark of my grandmother that it was Freud's presence, his being in the same room, above all, that had been effective; words were only of secondary importance". Perhaps Freud might be considered a relational psychoanalyst after all, who used his presence and his personality, as well as his extraordinary capacity for metaphor, symbolism, and interpretation, to forge meaningful communication with his patients.

We sense that the analysis proved helpful to Dr Guggenbühl and that as it neared its ending, she began to dread the termination of what we would now regard as a relatively short duration of treatment. In one of the last extracts, Dr Guggenbühl reported a dream, of which she wrote: "Fr. has stolen something". Might this be a reference to the patient's thought that Freud had taken away something very precious from Guggenbühl, having previously arranged to end her treatment entirely just prior to his summer holiday?

Not only does Anna Koellreuter's edition of her grandmother's diary contain a carefully translated, edited, and annotated text along with beautiful photographs of her family, as well as a reproduction of one of Freud's letters; but, also, we have the benefit of Koellreuter's own reminiscences and contextualisations. Koellreuter writes as both a loving granddaughter and as an experienced psychoanalyst, offering her own understanding of Freud's clinical technique. I particularly valued Koellreuter's classification of Freud's approach to the formulation of interpretations: "First, they are suggestive and leading; second, they are symbolistic; and third, they are reductive". Modern practitioners might approach the formulation of an interpretation with more delicacy and diplomacy and, perhaps, with less certitude; but one suspects that without Freud's pioneering approach to the rendering of the interpretation, our contemporary psychoanalytical discourse would be much poorer indeed.

As a welcome bonus, Koellreuter has commissioned three excellent chapters which complete the book, each written by intellectually robust and historically rigorous Continental psychoanalytical scholars: Professor Karl Fallend, Dr Ernst Falzeder (who had translated Koellreuter's original paper into English), and Professeur André Haynal.

First of all, Karl Fallend offers us a detailed contextualisation of the social and political climate at the time of Freud's analysis of Guggenbühl. Through his deft chapter, we learn of Freud's reliance on the fees of foreign patients who paid in Swiss francs or American dollars, which helped Freud to feed his family in the wake of the *Weltkrieg*. We also learn how Guggenbühl arrived in a post-war Vienna full of possibility, at a time when the feminist movement had begun to flourish, and when psychoanalysis became increasingly professionalised, institutionalised, and internationalised.

Ernst Falzeder has written a characteristically elegant chapter which surveys Freud's approach to clinical technique. Underscoring that Freud never succeeded in writing a comprehensive textbook of clinical rules, diaries such as Guggenbühl's assume a great importance in helping us to reconstruct his technical approach. Astutely, Falzeder underscores that this diary holds an important place as it constitutes one of the only detailed sources of Freud's working method prior to the onset of his cancer in 1923, which resulted in audiological problems for the founder of psychoanalysis. Reviewing Freud's many technical deviations (ranging from serving food to the "Rat Man", to offering money to Bruno Goetz, to walking round the Ringstraße with Dr Max Eitingon), Falzeder reminds us that for Freud, "It almost seems as if with him, these aberrations were not the exception, but the rule". Yet in spite of Freud's propensity for stretching his own rules, the Guggenbühl diary does, however, by contrast, provide us a glimpse of the more classical Freud who simply sat in his chair, "like an old owl in a tree" (H.D. [Hilda Doolittle], 1945, p. 85), rendering interpretations of dreams.

The book concludes with a helpful essay by André Haynal, a veritable *doyen* of Freud history, who has written a detailed study of the texture of Freud's work with Guggenbühl, underscoring how he helped his patient to feel understood and how he assisted Guggenbühl in broadening the focus of her analysis from her initial concerns to more characterologically-orientated issues.

It gives me great delight that English-speaking students of Freud and psychoanalysis now have the opportunity to enjoy this important primary document, presented in such a scholarly fashion; and it brings me much pleasure that we can include this volume in our "History of Psychoanalysis Series". Dr Anna Koellreuter could well have kept this private family diary under wraps for decades to come, but thanks to her generosity of spirit, those of us who still wish to learn from Sigmund Freud can now do so even more fully.

Professor Brett Kahr.
Series Co-Editor.
London.
June, 2016.

References

Anna G. [Anna Guggenbühl] (2010). *Mon Analyse avec le Professeur Freud.* Anna Koellreuter (Ed.). Jean-Claude Capèle (Transl.). Paris: Aubier/Flammarion, Aubier.

Cameron, Laura, and Forrester, John (1999). "A Nice Type of the English Scientist": Tansley and Freud. *History Workshop Journal, 48,* 62–100.

Cameron, Laura, and Forrester, John (2000). Tansley's Psychoanalytic Network: An Episode Out of the Early History of Psychoanalysis in England. *Psychoanalysis and History, 2,* 189–256.

Dorsey, John M. (1976). *An American Psychiatrist in Vienna, 1935–1937, and His Sigmund Freud.* Detroit, Michigan: Center for Health Education.

H.D. [Hilda Doolittle] (1945). Writing on the Wall. [Part I]. *Life and Letters To-Day, 45,* 67–98.

Kardiner, Abram (1977). *My Analysis with Freud: Reminiscences*. New York: W.W. Norton and Company.

Koellreuter, Anna (2007). Being Analysed by Freud in 1921: The Diary of a Patient. Ernst Falzeder (Transl.). *Psychoanalysis and History*, 9, 137–151.

Koellreuter, Anna (Ed.). (2009). *"Wie benimmt sich der Prof. Freud eigentlich?": Ein neu entdeckes Tagebuch von 1921 historisch und analytisch kommentiert.* Gießen: Psychosozial-Verlag.

Pohlen, Manfred (2006). *Freuds Analyse: Die Sitzungsprotokolle Ernst Blums.* Reinbeck bei Hamburg: Rowohlt/Rowohlt Verlag.

Roazen, Paul (1995). *How Freud Worked: First-Hand Accounts of Patients.* Northvale, New Jersey: Jason Aronson.

Wortis, Joseph (1954). *Fragments of an Analysis with Freud*. New York: Simon and Schuster.

The story of the diary

Anna Koellreuter

"What is this Professor Freud like, and how does he actually behave?" Anna Guggenbühl's father asks his daughter in a letter of 13 June 1921. From April to July 1921, Anna was in analysis with Freud, a period during which she did not write to her family at all. She did, however, keep a diary about her sessions.

The analysand is my grandmother. More than twenty-six years ago—seven years after she passed away—a letter from Freud was discovered when clearing her house. In this letter, Freud names the conditions to be fulfilled should an analysis take place: his fees, a minimum duration of four months, and the analysand's willingness to make a decision as soon as possible. Shortly after this discovery, we also found her diary. I was quite shaken by this find. My family and I have always been aware that my grandmother had been in analysis with Freud, even if she herself never talked about it in detail—not even to me. As a university student, I had lived with her and my grandfather for a couple of years while training in the same profession as she had, namely, psychoanalysis. In spite of her training, my grandmother had never practised. Even when she showed great interest in my analytical work, she always resisted addressing her own analysis with Freud. What exactly was taboo about it? Did she think that the analysis went well, or was the problem that she thought it didn't? Why didn't she practise as an analyst after working as a psychiatrist for several years, first at the Burghölzli in Zurich, and later in Paris? Did she never plan to do so in the first place? These and many other questions puzzled me.

Surprisingly, after having read the notebooks that contained the diary, I was hardly pleased with the sensational discovery. On the contrary, I mostly felt perplexed and biased; impressions that would affect me more strongly the more I read my grandmother's notes. The intimacy of what she recorded, and the unique expressions she chose, had something about them that scared me. At the same time, however, I was aware of how precious a find I had at hand here—the reactions it provoked in my immediate personal and professional surroundings only reaffirmed this. When I started speaking about the diary, I was immediately urged to make it accessible to the public, or to at least hand it over to the care of the Sigmund Freud Archives. The pressure from the outside grew to a degree that I decided to just leave the whole affair be. In addition, my family, at this point, was not prepared to give their consent to publication.

All these years, I could not stop thinking about the diary. I flipped through it time and again. At some point I started transcribing it, and finally reconsidered the possibility of publishing. My most important question was: How can I protect my grandmother, but still give the public access to her diary? In February 2007, I decided to give a talk about it at the symposium *Zur Geschichte der Psychoanalyse* [Towards the History of Psychoanalysis] in Tübingen, Germany. The response was overwhelming, and publication became a topical issue once again. I did not want to focus on my grandmother's life, so a biography was out of the question. Instead, I wanted the notes she took during her analysis with Freud to take centre stage—that is, I was interested in the insights into Freud's methods and ways of working that the diary could provide.

To me, the crucial question was: how can I, as a psychoanalyst, address a grandmother who was both a psychiatrist and in analysis with Freud? Many seemed to envy me for being granddaughter to one of Freud's patients. I was facing a dilemma. To the experts, the discovery of the diary is a sensation. To me, as an involved family member, it is also a problem—a problem that can be best summed up in the question I keep returning to; namely, the question whether this analysis was a success or not. I cannot answer this question, neither as a granddaughter, nor as a psychoanalyst. I cannot and do not want to treat my grandmother as a "case"—for this, I am too biased.

Finally, I had an idea of how to unburden myself: ask other people! In other words, show the diary to a number of experts in the fields of psychoanalytical historical studies and theory building, and invite them to share their thoughts on my grandmother's notes on her interaction with Freud. Since they do not know my grandmother, I reckoned, they would be able to engage with the records freely and without prejudice.

With this idea, I approached twenty authors. All of them were provided with the same material to work with: I sent them the paper I had given in Tübingen (2007), a complete transcript of the diary, and an article about my Tübingen talk that had been published in *Die Zeit* (Falzeder, 2007). I did not instruct them with questions or topics of my own. The authors were to go about their texts without restrictions or predetermination. Most of them were fascinated not only by access to the hitherto unknown diary the project promised, but also by the possibility of exploring it without topical restrictions. Many immediately agreed to contribute. The call resulted in an edited volume comprising sixteen very diverse articles that scrutinised the source text from a wide range of different perspectives.

The book was published in 2009 for the first time, with a second edition following in 2010. The year after the diary's first publication was eventful. Many presentations and book talks took place. The book was translated and published in French (Koellreuter, 2010). In the autumn of 2009, Peter Brunner of Sogar Theater Zurich produced a play reading of the diary notes, which sold out for eight evenings. The most recent play reading took place at the Leo Baeck Institute in New York on 21 May 2014.[1] Thanks to the brilliant performers Graziella Rossi and Helmut Vogel, I could finally *hear* the voice of the diary, namely that of my grandmother, for the first time after years of reading. This did not only touch me on a personal level in yet another new way, but also opened up new dimensions of the diary for me. Only now I am able to understand the three stages that followed my intense involvement with the diary of the analysis—and thus with my grandmother herself.

In the first stage, I was occupied with my basic initial problem: the fact that I could not, and did not want to, analyse the protocols myself. This resulted in the idea of letting others do the evaluating, and thus kick off a discussion about Freud's methods and ways of working. In a way, this also meant putting my grandmother in the hands of strangers.

While the contributions generated by this approach were as exciting and multifaceted as I had wished for them to be, they were partly also upsetting to me. After all, my grandmother was not always portrayed in the way I see her, or want her to be seen. The authors' contributions brought other aspects about my grandmother and her analysis to light. What was at stake in the book basically also threatened to question the relationship I had with my grandmother. But this was the price I had to pay for the publication.

The next stage, the book launch, allowed me to work through these grievances. As time went by, I was able to situate myself at a certain distance from the book, and thus appropriate the publication for myself. Thinking about the book to (and for) myself, I noticed that my grandmother's notes contained all the general topics of an analysis: Oedipus complex, sibling rivalry, symbolism, and so on. Her declarations of love to Freud become conscious quickly enough, as transference-love is part and parcel of every analysis. Freud can offer only a few new insights, because she had already read many of his texts. One could put it this way: she transports all the general material in her diary. But she also decided to take down and work through that which made her analysis particular, that is, everything that helped her become capable of loving and making the right decision. The reader remains excluded from these processes. This also applies to me, her granddaughter.

The third and (for now) last stage of appropriation was enabled by the theatrical reading of the diary, by actors, on stage. The discord I felt about the publication subsided when I could hear her voice, and that of Freud. The theatrical reading transmitted the formidable emotional oscillations between the two, generated by analysand and analyst engaging with each other in an erotic-narcissist fashion. The interpretation of her dreams, in the diary as well as on stage, reminded me that she gave me her own copy of Freud's *The Interpretation of Dreams* (1900a) as a gift when I was a teenager. And I finally realised how great her interest in dreams and their interpretation had been all through her life.

For this publication, four of the sixteen texts in the German volume have been selected to accompany the diary. My own contribution primarily focuses on Freud's methods, which appear—at least in my grandmother's memories—suggestive in the sense that Freud's conviction of the Oedipus complex's universal effectuality at times made him lead his analysand's associations in his favoured direction, instead of following them.

After my diary story, there is a fully translated version of the diary itself, edited by Ernst Falzeder. Following that is a chapter that offers a small collection of visual material relating to Anna Guggenbühl's life and diary. Three further contributions complete the volume.

Karl Fallend's chapter, "'Prof. Freud calls for tolerance!' Dashes that moved the couch—and politics", describes the development of psychoanalysis in the light of the political upheavals in post-war Vienna. Based on a number of early diary entries (*"the sounding of the flute"*) that mention Arthur Schnitzler's novella *The Shepherd's Pipe*, Karl Fallend illustrates the political climate of this particular period, which stretched well into Anna Guggenbühl's analysis. Schnitzler's scandalous play *La Ronde* was a scorching critique of bourgeois sexual morality, a critique that Freud shared with the playwright: "Marital unfaithfulness would ... be a much more probable cure for the neurosis resulting from marriage" (Freud, 1908d, p. 23).

Ernst Falzeder's text discusses Freud as analyst and therapist. Drawing on Freud's own texts, memoirs of and interviews with former analysands, reports in secondary literature, and the information pro-vided by Freud's patient calendars, Falzeder traces Freud's methods, and describes him as a creative, highly flexible analyst, whose work at times also covered psychotherapeutic terrain in a narrower sense.

André Haynal's contribution reads Anna Guggenbühl's analysis as displaying methods that would be regarded as classic in the decades that followed. He argues that all basic ideas *and* the limitations of these methods become apparent in the notes. In effect, André Haynal's article provides a supervision of Freud's methods from today's point of view. Freud takes a position of power, that of the savant, and appears doctri-nal. The theoretical problems that occupied him at the time clearly push through. In other words: the analysis shows the dynamics of a counter-transference that could not be openly addressed, and thus also points towards the mysterious connections between an analyst's autoanalysis and their analysis of the patient. Haynal argues that these are crucial dimensions of present-day psychoanalytical practice.

I would like to thank the following people. My family's consent was a prerequisite for the publication of the diary. I am particularly indebted to my mother, Anne Roth-Huggler, and her brothers and sister, who entrusted me with the care of the original diary notebooks. I am infinitely grateful to Graziella Rossi, Helmut Vogel, and Peter Brunner of Sogar Theater Zurich, who, as performers and dramatic adviser, brought the diary to life. Finally, I would like to thank Kristina Pia Hofer in Vienna, who translated the texts and the diary from German to English in the shortest time imaginable.

Note

1. How is this Professor Freud, and how does he actually behave? Diary of an analysis with Dr Sigmund Freud. Performed by Graziella Rossi and Tom Regan (stand-in for Helmut Vogel). Music: Harry White, saxophone.

References

Falzeder, E. (2007). "Sie streifen so nah am Geheimnis." Eine kleine wissenschaftliche Sensation: Das bislang unbekannte Tagebuch einer Freud-Patientin, die ihre Sitzungen protokollierte. *Die Zeit*, 2 August, p. 32.

Freud, S. (1900a). *The Interpretation of Dreams. S. E.*, 4–5. London: Hogarth.

Freud, S. (1908d). "Civilized" Sexual Morality and Modern Nervous Illness. *S. E., 9*: 179. London: Hogarth.

Koellreuter, A. (2007). Als Patientin bei Freud 1921. Aus dem Tagebuch einer Analysandin. *Werkblatt. Zeitschrift für Psychoanalyse und Gesellschaftskritik, 58*(1): 3–23.

Koellreuter, A. (Ed.) (2010). *Mon analyse avec le Professeur Freud—Anna G.* Paris: Aubier/Flammarion.

Schnitzler, A. (1911). *Die Hirtenflöte*. Stuttgart: Deutscher Bücherbund, 1975.

CHAPTER ONE

Diary of an analysis, April 1921*

First book

(no date, i.e., at the beginning)

Page (1)

When I was four years old, in Strasbourg, there was my little cousin, a fat baby. I pinched her, and when I was alone I always bullied her until she cried. Once I pulled out all the saplings on the balcony, I thought they were weeds. Incidentally, I discovered masturbation there by pressing myself against a cornice.

Fr [Freud]: This is a very remarkable memory. Did you also badger your little brother?

I turned him on his back, for instance, so that he could no longer get up.

Fr: You started to masturbate when you felt lonely. You were no longer loved[1]

---

*Translation: Ernst Falzeder and Kristina Pia Hofer.

(2)

as much as when you were as a single child. So you took revenge on the little child and on the symbol, the sapling.

When my brother Walter was born, I asked when I saw him: Why doesn't he cry?

Fr: ["]So you would have liked to see him in a crying state, just like your cousin?"

--------------------[2]

One can clearly see three levels in your life:
The uppermost one is your present conflict with R etc.
The one in the middle concerns your relation to your brother.
You are still quite unconscious of the deepest level, which is connected with your parents,

(3)

and which is the most important one. It is from this that the relation to the brother is derived.

--------------------[3]

Later. I tell Freud: When I went to grammar school, I thought I would like to love a young man who was immensely sad, and I would make life possible for him, and he then would be happy.

Fr: Like with your brother.

Then I thought later I would like to have seven children; I did not think of the father.

Fr: Seven men, actually. Seven?

Adam had seven sons.[4] Papedöne[5] hangs

(4)

his seven sons. *Der Hungerueli Isegrind frisst sini 7 chline Chind.*[6] I believe male cats devour their offspring.

Fr: You are coming so near the secret of the deepest level that I can break it to you:

You loved your father, and never forgave him his betrayal with the mother. You wanted to be the mother of the child. So you wished the mother, who took the lover away from you ~~for herself~~, dead. Bit by bit you will produce evidence for this, and the riddle of why you cannot get away from your brother will be solved.

----

(5)

Three layers are easily recognisable in your life, the present one, which concerns the brothers; and the deepest one, which is connected with the parents. What is pathological is the long-lasting indecision whether or not you should marry Richard. The fact that no decision is reached proves that something else must lie behind it, something that is, as you recognise yourself, connected with the brothers and the parents.

"In Paris, I liked Walter ~~so much~~; suddenly he, and no longer Adolf, seemed to be my ideal.["]

"You glide from one to the other, just as you do with the lovers. The lovers are brother substitutes, that's why they are of the same age, actually younger in a social sense.["]

(6)

I'd like to go to Russia; like those aristocratic sons and daughters who left their families during the last revolution, I'd like to go away and leave the milieu into which I do not belong. I am thinking of that piece by Schnitzler, "*Der Flötenton* ('The Sounding of the Flute').["][7]

"That is exactly your conflict.["][8]

(7) 15 April, 21

I had two dreams: A schizophrenic man was there and my mother and my grand-mother, and it was unpleasant.
Then there was another dream: A stocking made of brocade, blue and embroidered with gold, but embroidered in a careless way, it was cheap brocade, the threads were sticking out so much.[9]

What comes to your mind concerning the schizophrenic?

I once believed Richard to be schizophrenic, when we took a walk on a meadow and when he suddenly, in the middle of an important conversation, looked at the horses, I thought: Now he is obstructed.[10] Hans Peter,[11] however, ~~was~~ is in fact schizophrenic.

(8)

Immer,[12] too. I also believed that the sculptor's family was schizoid, because one brother is a teacher and does not want to marry, and one sister, over 30, is also unmarried. When Adolf had the neurosis, I thought I wanted to learn psychoanalysis,[13] if only he were able to last for a few more years; because I love him so much, my accomplishments will be so much greater than those of any other human being. ~~On~~ Then with Richard I thought again, I want to learn everything, so that I can figure everything out. Now, I am learning it for my own sake.

"Stocking?"

I believe a condom is called Parisian stocking. It was embroidered in a rough way, in cheap brocade,

(9)

just like a small purse I wanted to give my cousin for Christmas. In artificial light it looked quite nice, but in daylight it was cheap. I later exchanged it for a nicer purse.

"So the masculine symbol is substituted for a female one—a purse.["]

I used to be jealous of[14] this cousin. She planned to also go to Geneva, and I imagined the possibility of Richard falling in love with her. I thought: She must die, and I thought it possible to kill her by my wishing her dead.

"Blue and gold?"

Blue and gold was the little purse my brother gave to Helen. He also gave her a stocking full of presents. Every morning he gave

(10)

her something else. One time it was a jewel case, another time an apple made of wax. Jéwel cases are my biggest pleasure, I have a collection of them. Actually the one that Dölf gave Helen was not so nice; I found a lovely one in Paris, which I wanted to give to Helen. But I did not have the heart to do it.

"Did you think it might bring her bad luck?"

Yes. Once I believed my mother was a witch, when I was about 18 years old and I screamed in the night, she came to my bed in a nightgown. Not an ordinary witch. Once when I was a child I dreamed[15] that my great-grandmother was made of wax. She was of wax and turned around

(11)

That is the most ghastly thing. Once I visited a trade show with my other grand-mother and I was looking through a glass. I saw a man standing on the footboard of a coach. He was murdering somebody. Was he called Dreifuss? It was ghastly. So sculptural, like made of wax.

Freud: last time we saw that you are bored, that you would like to love somebody. Now there are two ways in analysis: Some people have to do everything, the others, where enough mental material is present, deal with everything within their psyche. If possible, put a stop to the adventures. Bear it and suffer want, so that everything will come out all the more clearly

(12)

in the analytic hour.

18 April, 21

1st dream: I was lying in bed in the evening, the light was on. Then I saw, on the left side of my head, disgusting, brownish stains on the sheet. Repellent little worms moved in the liquid (they [the stains] still wet). I was disgusted and called my dad, and he was there and just laughed a bit, he was not frightened. It was like when I was a child and was scared and he came.
2nd dream: Helen was wearing an embroidered dress and asked me: Do you like it?

(13)

I said: Yes, it is wonderful!, but the dress was not so beautiful, I just pretended. Helen however had actually meant to ask if I liked a particular carpet, which was also embroidered. The carpet was indeed more beautiful than the dress and would have better fitted my answer, but the embroidery was still rather coarse, looking slightly Bulgarian, not new.

Freud: "It is more appropriate to look at the 2nd, more recent dream first. Again, it contains a speech. Usually, the words are taken from a speech in reality."[16]

At Christmas, a year ago, my cousin had embroidered a handkerchief for my mother, and I said: It is delightful, although I did not like it. My brother later said: You have

(14)

come quite far in pretending. When Helen was in Paris, I also pretended to like her coat, when she asked me what I thought of it. I did not like it as much as I said when I first looked at it.

Fr: Thus the embroidered handkerchief and the coat have condensed into the embroidered dress.

To my dismay, I was quite satisfied in Paris that Helen was not as elegant as I managed to be. Back home, when I made a show of my dresses, Dölf and Richard became sad, and so did I, because my mischievous purpose had achieved its end: to stir Dölf's admiration and to intimidate Richard.

(15)

Carpet: The Smyrna[17] carpet in the oriel has brownish stains from the coffee that Dölf (her brother) and his friends drank there.

Fr: "So they are a bridge to the first dream, to the brownish stains."

When I went to a café with the sculptor in my new dress, a young artist spilled coffee on my dress. I smiled and said: No problem.
Once the sculptor embraced me. Afterwards there were stains on my dress, but it was a different dress. He was terribly sorry, but I said: no problem, really.

Fr: "So in the dream you call your father for help against the aggressions of the young men

(16)

You take refuge in your father. Your unconscious thus confirms my statement that your father was your first lover. Have you read the study on a hysteric: Dora?[18] *(Yes, but I don't remember anything) Your dream is completely modeled on Dora's one. So you take the place of Dora, who, as we know, is in love with her father. At first there comes the intellectual willingness, then one accepts evidence from the unconscious, only then one admits it emotionally, and finally, as a conclusion, direct memories appear. Your love of the brother, conscious as it is, is not the deepest layer, and thus the knowledge*

(17)

of its existence is useless, you cannot free yourself from it, because it has deeper roots.

19 April, 21

When I think "carpet," I think of a carpet of flowers. I had a dream that when I was in Teufen,[19] I fall into an abyss, and when I hit the ground I was lying on a wealth of forget-me-nots (+ dream of the old woman). In Teufen, I was terribly homesick.

When I was not yet 4 years old, my mother often took me along to see my grand-parents in Aussersihl.[20] We walked in an alley lined with chestnut trees (Gessnerallee[21]) and she pushed the carriage with little Adolfli. I heard the trains whistle and I was homesick, I was alone.

(18)

Freud: Was your father traveling often? So you were homesick for him.

In the recreation home in Enge,[22] too, I was so homesick that he came on Sundays; I was crying the whole day because he was leaving again. Once, when I was a child of about 10 years, I imagined how it might be to sleep with him, but just as a game, without desire.—~~I am surprised, however, that~~[23]

The great-grandmother turning to wax all of a sudden. This song in Faust always seemed so familiar, morbid: "There sits my mother upon a stone, and her head is wagging ever."[24] It is similar.

Besides: I have murdered my mother, and my child

(19)

I drowned.

<u>Fr</u>: *The "turning to wax," i.e., the death of the great-grandmother, is a substitute for the death of the mother that is wished for.*

When I sprained my knee, I thought: It is like with my brother, who sprained his foot after his *Matura*[25] when he actually wanted to amuse himself; but it is definitely a punishment because I wished upon Richard's sister to have a stiff knee. She was in opposition to my love, i.e., engagement.

Fr: The unconscious confirms after the fact that she was right and said: since I no longer love Richard, she had been jinxed in vain.

Me: She behaved the same way toward

(20)

Richard: When he was expelled from the fraternity she did not want to associate with him anymore. He wanted to take his own life and sat on a rock on the riverside of the Aare.[26] Then an elderly gentleman came along who addressed him, it was as if he knew about everything.

Fr: So your fiancé, too, sits on a rock to die. Thus you are transferring the death wishes onto this area.

I keep thinking ["]he must die["] and ["]I must die["] in turns.

(21)

21. IV. 21

Dream:
Friends of Adolf and Walti [her brothers] were there, but they were all a bit younger. They swam out into the lake, and the sun was shining. Oesch [one of the friends] was there and he was very little, I help him get over the wall, because he couldn't do it on his own, and in the garden on the other side he suddenly threw himself on me and embraced me. I was a bit surprised that such a little boy dared do that and I didn't really like it because there were people who were watching. Then I had a sweet little jewel case. I said: The lid looks like a chessboard, but when I opened it it was not like a chessboard at all. There were the loveliest things in it,

(22)

for example, a little wedding party, little people cut out of paper so they could stand up. I wi wanted to give some to Margrit, but I regretted it.

Fr: The many friends

They were all little, almost like children, Oesch in part.[icular] was very little. I helped him get over the wall, that is, I seduced him to love.

[27]*Fr: Let us insert the symbols that we know thanks to our insights*

Chessboard: My father recently said he had played chess with my mother before they became engaged, and then he had asked her whether she wanted to be his queen.

Fr: ["]You can also insert the symbols yourself, so that you can make a connection when

(23)

you get stuck with the associations. ~~Rampart~~ *Wall—this is the wall that has to be surmounted to embrace you." It is the hymen. The little jewel case is the*[28] *genital.*

Fr: The dream beautifully shows ~~how~~ *the tendencies from the past. The jewel case is like a chessboard, i.e. you are taking the place of the mother, but afterwards: it is no chessboard after all, meaning, you turn away from the father. The friends, the "little ones," swimming around there, are symbols for the male member. You help him surmount the wall, that means, you want a real defloration that eventually leads to marriage (the little wedding party in the box)*

(24)

You begrudge your cousin Margrit the marriage. The sun always stands for the father.[29]

The sun was shining the same way in 2 other dreams: I. I was lying in bed in the morning and the sun was shining through the patio door, beautifully. Then the friends of Adolf came in, Walti, too, he put a book on the cover. I told them to leave the room again because of mother. II. Dream from grammar school: I sat at the kitchen table, sun was shining through the window beautifully, I had a young lilac twig in my hand, with young green leaves. They were not yet

(25)

in bloom. The table is the mother. I am thinking of mother making small cakes for Carnival on the white table that is covered in flour. "At

Carnival my mother bakes/delicious little cakes./But then my dad comes running,/and steals the cakes with cunning.["][30]

Fr: You are sitting on a table: like a little cake, these little cakes are the children which are made by the mother.

Me: The father eats the cakes just like the Hungerueli Isegrind devours his 7 children.

Twig: One time, a dog ran after me. I had to throw him autumn twigs from a bunch I carried so that he would not bite me. It was like the story of the wolves

(26)

in Russia, which are running after the sleigh, and blankets are thrown at them, etc.
One time when I was about 9 years old I walked home from school and a boy was beating our[31] fox terrier with a little rod. I slapped him in the face. Afterwards he and his mother came to our home and accused me. Only my grandmother was present. She wanted to drag me out onto the little patio, so that I should apologise to the boy in front of all the people who had gathered in front of the garden. I did not do it but she dragged me out together with the maid.

(27)

22. IV. 21

The little rod is a divining rod (the lilac twig from the last dream). A little rod as the water diviners[32] use it.

Fr: Do you perhaps remember that during masturbation you imagined children being beaten?[33]

I imagined myself being beaten by the imaginary man. Once, but only once, when Papa threatened to beat Adolf as soon as we were home, I had a feeling of revulsion combined with some interest, but it was gone when the threat was put into action. It was, after all, only the threat.

When resistances arise in the analysis you behave in a similar way because I am representing the father; the idea that the cure is of no avail, for

(28)

Fr: This is the wish of being beaten yourself, because this means for the girl (child) to be loved in a sexual way. Out of the desire for love + the guilty conscience. Later on it takes the form of wishing to be merely scolded. When resistances arise in the analysis, you behave in a similar way because I am representing the father. p.ex.[34] the idea that the cure is of no avail is already the beginning of that. Your anxiety that you might make an even more stupid choice in your marriage afterwards, because you wouldn't be able to endure it, is baseless, because the purpose of the cure is precisely to enable you to control that instinct and thus to be able to make a free choice of whom to marry,

(29)

and not out of fear of the instinct. This objection is reminiscent of the story of the goose keeper and the horse keeper, who plan what they would do if they hit the jackpot.[35] The horse keeper describes the palace he would live in, the servants, etc. The goose keeper said he would thereupon only ever herd his geese from horseback.
The idea that you ħ would be too old to start a new life is all the more unjustified in that you prolonged your puberty to an extraordinary degree by your studies, and that you have had very little experience.

At Burghölzli[36] there was a girl

(30)

who was very intelligent and had a fine grasp of psycholog.[ical] understanding, she was called Anna[37]
She wanted to ~~herself~~ learn stenography, but she did not get past the very first page, she could not focus at all.
I, too cannot focus any more.

Fr: Aha a Swiss national diagnosis!

[38](31) (32) (33)

(34)

25 April.

When Goethe was pretty[39] old he wanted to marry a girl.[40] In the past I thought that she, of course, did not like the idea, but now I see quite well that one might want to marry someone older. So t.[his] m.[eans] I might per.[haps] want to marry you, I really like you very much.

Fr: Now this is the transference of the old love and infatuation you had for the father, onto me. All the painf.[ul] disappointment, jealousy etc. will come to light later, too.

(35)

26 April, 21

In the waiting room I heard the pat.[ient] who comes before me say the word "chlorophyll." I thought I could never come up with such an association. I am so terribly ignorant. I lack all humanistic education, and I haven't absorbed the scientific education either.

Fr: So you want to belittle yourself intellectually. Other women usually do it in physical matters. They might for instance say they've got haemorrhoids,[41] etc.

Pause, nothing comes to mind.

Fr: so this is a spec.[ial] resistance that has to do with transference.

I cannot tell you how much I like you; I think I've never loved anybody this way before.

(36)

Fr: This love for your father was so enormous that everything that came later paled in comparison. People have no idea of the intensity of the love of children, it only exists in potential form, after all, and is not put into action.

When I was a child I always thought: Let me never experience unhappy love, for my love is greater than that of other people.

Fr: You are able to think all that only because you had already experienced disappointment at one time, which you did not remember ~~consciously~~. When you belittle yourself you do so to spoil your love for <u>me</u>, just like e.g. the lady with the haemorrhoids

"But why does a neurosis then develop in me, is it not so that all human beings experience such disappointment.["]

(37)

Fr: First of all, the force of passion varies in different persons. There is a degree of passion that can no longer be dealt with by the child, secondly, the other party's behaviour can be a cause.

26 April, 21

Dream: In three parts.

1. I am sitting on the water closet and many people are present. I cannot pass t.[he] urine and am finally getting up again because I don't quite like having so many people watching me.
2. I am sitting on the water closet and a man, maybe a Spaniard, stands in the door, pushing to get in. I catch his finger by slamming the door shut.

(38)

3. Uncle Arthur says about Richard: He is really a good person and not very intelligent. (So that the 2 parts do not quite match. It should rather say: "but")[42]

Ad. 2:

The Spaniard puts his finger in the crack of the door and I catch it: Richard once told me about 2 lovers who froze to death in a cold winter night because the man could not withdraw his penis.
Water closet: There was a case in my final exam: a girl aborted a child, which then fell into the toilet[43] as a premature baby, about 7 months old.

Fr: Premature birth = toilet.[44] The toilet is thus the visual symbol of the abortion.

Margrit's fiancé had something to do with an abortion, in which he

(39)

played a questionable part. Richard, too, in another abortion, in which he proved how unreliable he was. Spaniard—or Hungarian.

Yesterday I went to a café with a Hungarian, who left the boarding house today.

~~Fr:~~

Concerning the 1st dream: As a boy Dölf was afraid of the water gushing in the toilet, but I wasn't. He believed a water nymph was in there.

Fr: The sound of the water reminded him of the sound his mother caused when urinating, which he witnessed as a little child. Water nymph = mother symbol/ naked woman in the water. For obvious reasons you did not need to be afraid. The first dream is simply an

(40)

illustration of you yourself as a woman. You sit down for passing your water. The feeling of being embarrassed is in the background. That you think of the brother's fear of the sound of water in this instance points at it. The second part is like a description out of a novel. In the dream, the Hungarian has become the drama's romantic protagonist. You want to hold on to him.
The 3rd part clearly culls from the uppermost level.

Assoc.[iation] from feeling embarrassed f.[or] water closet: Papa was always embarrassed when we burst into the bedroom and he was changing, for instance. On the other hand he would not be embarrassed of coming into my bedroom while I was getting changed for the night. In my puberty I was much irritated by that. I thought that he might have

(41)

~~sexu~~ erot.[ic] feelings towards[45] me

27.

Dream:
Some little friend of Walter was a little fond of me, probably embraced me.

Then I was with Papa on a straight country road. I wondered whether I should hang my coat in a narrow cabinet or not. Eventually I hung my coat, an umbrella and another small object in the cabinet, and went for a walk with Papa on the straight country road, in the sun, without any clothes on. Then people were coming and I was ashamed of my nakedness

(42)

and also because there I had something about me that was not quite right; I think I had ugly high shoulders, something vulgar.
I was in a hotel at nightfall. There was something about a bill I had to pay, and my cousin Margrit was there, too.
The little one represents the penis, i.e. I have intercourse with my father.
~~Is~~
The cabinet stood in the anatomy department [of the university], back then, I always used to meet Richard at that cabinet. I really did put my coat, my umbrella and my notebook inside. One time he thought I had lost his notebook, he made a scene, it turned out it was not true, he had

(43)

mislaid it himself. He conducted himself quite badly this time.

Fr: The father and Richard thus melt into one person in the dream. You are dissatisfied with Richard.

I have a high shoulder bl[ades]: My friend Hedwig in Paris was not such a pretty[46] sight. I saw her when she was ill and I thought I could not possibly love her. Also, that such an unattractive body could not be a coincidence. I myself have beautiful round shoulders. In the dream, therefore, there is something vile about me.
Country road—In the country road dream I had as a child it was the same straight road. To the left and to the right there was a swamp and many hands wanted to pull me into it—I thought this was about my masturbation

(44)

The hotel is a brothel. During masturbation I imagined being in a house with other girls like me. An unknown man beat me and had intercourse with me.

Fr: And who might this unknown man be?

The father

When we moved into the house where we live now, said [sic]: how pleasant, it is just like a hotel. Adolf had had the same idea about the other house: the corridor looked like out of a brothel to us, even though we had never seen one before.
His lover, who was very erotic, would later become a prostitute. I thought that if I was just like her, i.e. if I had her success and at the same time had my own

(45)

efficiency, I would have everything. Cousin Margrit is merely beautiful; but I have a better character, more energy, or so I thought.

*Fr: The coat and the umbrella are symbols—*I know.—*Fr: So this means that you take off your masculinity, and are proud of being a woman, but later are ashamed again of being a woman. You have a strong masculinity complex.*
Maybe you regretted being a girl when your brother was born, after all, you said your father loved him very much, that he actually liked him best.

(46)

30 April, 21

A man, probably of ill character, a Don Juan, that's what he is. Concerning cousin Margrit or Anni Scheidegger I say: Basically every human heart is a leaf of lilac.[47] With this I mean to say that there is something good in every human being.
Adolf gave Helen a ring of jade, with a stone in the shape of a leaf or a heart.

Fr: You are the Don Juan.

Dream: I am in a mine. A young [female] doctor tells me about her sister who is also a young doctor, that she is married and has 7 intelligent boys and a paralyzed girl. I am not surprised about this. "With her intelligence you should have expected it." I say. On the way home Papa or Mama say: You should not tell everybody that you and Richard are so poor so that you cannot eat nuts anymore. I say: But in psychoanalysis I am also telling everything, and in any case I've given up those prejudices by now.

A thug is sought by warrant by the police, and two officers are looking for him. Sometimes he dresses up

(48)

as a woman, sometimes as a man. Finally he is caught, and the description on the warrant fits. It also says there that he is cross-eyed. He really is cross-eyed. The officer asks him: Do you squint to the left or to the right? The thug always squints to the opposite side, so that the stupid officer cannot arrest him.

Mama, thinking that I was in love with this Merian[48] was actually a quite accomplished idea of mine!
Analysis:
The mine is the underground of the soul, the unconscious. The [female] doctor and her sister are both me. I wanted to have 7 boys and I thought I should also have a girl. Lately I decided to stop fantasising about the future children, so that I would not be disappointed. Probably I'll get what I would want the least: A daughter who sits quietly on a chair and does the mending and shows no interest in the world. Who is, in fact, paralyzed.
The thug is the resistance. He dresses up as he likes, as a man or as a woman, corresponding with the so-called masculinity complex. Squints to the right or to the left: Riklin[49] said I should detach myself from my mother, and you say from my father. You and Riklin are the stupid officers. ~~When you of the detach~~ So the thug evades the situation by squinting to the opposite side, at this moment in squinting to the mother, because you always want to uncover the romantic relations to the father.

(50)[50]

This Merian, I did not like the merest bit. Especially when he sent me a letter in which he wrote about nothing but the weather, and in a very, very unintelligent way at that.
The sculptor too wrote a stupid letter, which sobered me.

Fr: So the men do not come off well in this dream. Perhaps it announces that you now want to resuscitate the homosexual component.

A different dréam: I am meeting Gertrud Birnstiel[51], I am in foreign town, and I tell her that the doctor in the *Versorgungshaus*[52] had suggested to have my meniscus removed after all. The operation will take place tomorrow. I am

(51)

very scared that my knee will go septic and remain stiff. For God's sake, I wouldn't be able to dance anymore. T. Birnstiel says that this is an ill-advised agreement that should be called off, and that I would surely have to stay in the hospital for 2 months. "I cannot stand this," but I know that it is already too late, everything has been arranged.

Analysis:
I am concerned that after my analysis men will not fall in love with me any longer, dancing and loving is the same. Even now I cannot do without someone who likes me. I figured out that the analysis will only go on for about 2 more months (mid-July) It appears as if

(52)

coming here was a delusional idea of mine. It is with difficulty that I remember that I had no choice.

4 May

Dream:

I had a prominent red blotch in the face. A [female] friend asked me: Is the blotch from your lover's kisses? I replied: No, from bugs. I squeezed it and slowly something grey came out from pressing it. I thought, if only this would not deform me forever.—

Analysis: I really have red blotches and bumps[53] from the bug bites, and yesterday I thought: I am like the convicts in the "resurrection"[54] <u>fodder for the lice</u>

Second book

(1)

May 4 (Continued from first book)

After all, I, too, am lonely and imprisoned. Instead of being lovingly devoured by the lover, the bugs are devouring me.

There was a girl at Burghölzli before I left. The girl that Bleuler[55] diagnosed as: stubborn harlot. She had a one-sided infection of the knee joint caused by gonorrhea, and Bl.[euler] said: If the gonococci would only devour such a woman!
In the dre am I wish to be punished for my sins: Should[56] ~~to~~ the vermin devour me!

Fr[57]: In addition to that, the dream also has a deeper meaning. When you squeeze the red swelling—does this remind you of something

Mitesser.[58]—Vermin is the symbol for children.

Freud: Mitesser is also a good expression for it, and is quite frequently found. At first one feeds it from what we eat ourselves, and finally the children devour us, that is, everything we own. The fear of

(2)

being disfigured by children is also justified when bearing numerous children.

This morning I pricked my finger, there was a drop of blood, and I thought this meant that I wanted to have a child. Snow White's mother pricked her finger when sewing, and wished for a child.[59]

Fr: Since the libido is dammed up because it cannot reach the man, all these wishes are surfacing more urgently here. This is also the purpose of abstinence.

5 May

In the dream I love a man I think he strongly resembles the sculptor and I ask him where he is from. He says: from Brienz[60] and I think: obviously I have a particular fondness for people from Brienz. I know, however, that in principle I am loving Richard [the fiancé, AK] and somehow this isn't right.

Analysis: I have a particular fondness for people

(3)

from certain areas: from Luxembourg, for example. I knew an intern at the Burghölzli, but When I was 19[61] years old, I got to know a Norwegian at a skiing course, whom I found very attractive, then again a similarly attractive Swede in Paris. I also like men from Basel, actually no longer quite so (listing t.[he] various). Once I thought I liked the Dutch. But I think that, although they are reliable and faithful, they are quite limited. I wouldn't like to marry a Frenchman.

Freud: This is quite a Leporello's aria, as in Don Juan. Catalogue Aria is what it's called. So my idea that in the dream you present yourself as a counterpart to Don Juan was right after all.

I believe this is why I am scared of cats: I remember that once a child touched me with the fur of a cat at t.[he] genitalia, a kind of masturbation.

Then, when I held the cat

(4)

on my lap I suddenly pressed it against me. I was aware of the underlying intention and I thought: what if it understood me and I was afraid when I caught its eyes.

When Adolf broke with Ruth, he asked me one day: Do you also believe that it is necessary? I

said: Yes, I am certain. He told her on the very same day, and I heard him cry in his room. It broke my heart.[62] That night I had a dream: Grandpapa (who, in reality, had died about half a year before) was lying in the bed all yellow, a dying man. I stepped to the bed and I strangled him. He knew what I was up to and looked at me with his eyes, terrible, but I did it all the same. When I woke up I had to cry and I thought this meant that it was me who dealt the deathly blow to Adolf's dying love. The eyes were ghastly. it [sic] was like the fear of the cat's glare, where I was also afraid that it might understand me.

Fr: This dream seems extreme—

(5)

ly important to me.[63]

(6) (7) (8) (9) (10) (11) (12) (13) (14)

[64]I am withdrawing from F.

(15)

Dream: I attend a lecture about
Autochists

Comp.[osite] of | masochist
                | autist perh. auto-erotists

Today I am dancing in front of the mirror as I did as a child because I am on my own again.

Fr: You felt sorry for your brother who was beaten by the father, (actually at first you had the wish to be in his place.) All these objects, the maimed,[65] are substitutes i.[n] p.[part] ~~but i~~ Now that you[66] are withdrawing your libido from Fr., this compassion turns onto yourself (auto-, masochist [)]. Your enormous compassion was originally directed toward yourself. That means that you can control this excessive compassion for the others, as it principally derives from the ego. You were the wronged one. The mother had the child instead of you.
Then all the same[67] you wanted to be like the brother. Either to be a woman and have a child or to be a man with the penis. In the ~~dee~~ still deeper layer the small is the same: child/penis[68]

(16)

You really got the short end of the stick, both lit.[erally] and fig.[uratively], that is why you pity all the maimed[69] part[icularly] the castrated, i.e. ~~only~~ e.g. the blind [70]d like Fr.[71] the one-eyed (goddess with one arm missing[72]) The immense desire to be a man resp.[ectively] to posses a penis shows in this[73] compulsion to fall in love.

The material is like tuff,[74] from which those wonderful Roman buildings are made, solidified lava, from which everything can be made Only that there is an eruption from time to time, since it is a volcano. Enormous passions but also an extraordinary sobrieties [sic].
Clear as mountain water[75]

(17)

Dream: 10 June
France[76] gives me saccharin. I say: Thank you, I'm passing.

Dream of 11 June.

I am sitting in an express train, which enters a big station in a foreign town. People are shouting: Boche, sale boche![77] I think: this happens to me for the first time. Then I am in the customs office with Adolf, there is a crowd. Behind me [78] sits an elderly blind man who presses me against him I have an uncomfortable feeling and I believe Adolf says: When he keeps his eyes wide open, opens them wide, one does not see that he is blind (he does it on purpose in order to dissimulate). Later we are back with a [female] officer in the customs office and we look for my coat, which got lost. It is very dear to me, but we do not find it. Adolf is I think a little inept.

(18)

Then we are at home, probably in the apartment Weinbergstr[asse] 1[79] or perhaps even earlier and Berta helps looking for the coat. I am glad I call her "Du"[80] but the coat is not to be found.

1.)

So I take a pass on the sugar substitute, i.e. on the caresses, which are[81] only a substitute themselves.

2.)

The people shout sale boche! i.e. what these Slovenes do not like in me, they see this piece of resistance or self control as a characteristic of the boche, a practical soul, who is incapable of flying high. Sale—France let me know that his comrades consider me to be the mistress of S. [sic] or of himself.
The man who sits behind me is my father castrated apparently as a punishment for the embrace. When he opens his eyes wide one cannot see that he is blind. In reality my father cannot in fact open his eyes

(19)

wide.

I am looking for my coat, that is, for my masculinity, per.[haps] the for a man.
Berta loved my brother more because he was a boy.
Why does she help me

Then I dreamed[82] a steam fly[83] was on the ceiling high above me and I was afraid it might fall down on me. I was lying in bed. Freud was there, too.

The steam fly is a child, namely—"From Heaven Above to Earth I Come"[84]—a Baby Jesus,[85] conceived from God. France commented my concern that the semen might penetrate the fabric by saying that this would be procreation by the Holy Ghost. The steam fly is thus also of him. He is just as big. Or the beetle is big because it is supernatural, being a child of the H[o]l[y] Ghost.

It is also my father's child, because Fr. is in the room as a father substitute.

(20)

14 June

Dream:
2 little boys jump about in a garden bordering a steep slope ~~in~~. There also were stalactite grottos—I was afraid they might ~~over~~ slip.

A lady asked me where I stayed, she was youthful, blond, a bit rouged. I told her about the boarding house Döbling.[86] Then ~~I saw~~ I was told that she herself was the manager of that boarding house, who is much older [in reality]. I was disgusted by this pretence, and wondered why I had not recognised her in spite of it. But not even my grandmother had recognised her. (In the dream she was alive) Then I looked at the lady, took off the pince-nez and looked at her through the lorgnette.

(21)

The 2 lit.[tle] boys are the male member.

Fr: Duplication often indicates castration.

I am afraid that t.[he] penis o.[f] France might slide into my vagina. As a punishment he is castrated. The lady looks like Minka,[87] blond, slightly rouged. Also Richard's sister, who play-acted a lot.

Fr: In fact it was you yourself who turned a "wrong" face toward Minka.

In the dream I turn this around. The manager of the boarding house is my mother, who here enters as a rival. ~~The~~
"Neither did the Grandmama see through the (my) disguise": Once, when I was with her, about 5 years old, I was at Ernst Israel's[88] in the garden. At night, just before bedtime. In the shed he lifted my dress and touched me. When I came upstairs Grandmama said: What have you done? I realised that she knew everything, although I could not

explain how she could have seen down into the shed from the veranda. Yesterday France embraced me on the stairs in front of the boarding house, which is also entwined by vine

(22)

leaves.
"So the Grandmama had already figured ~~the~~ my behaviour out" is in reverse in the dream, as the pretence is passed from my person to the other part.
~~Yesterday~~ Today there was another love scene between Fr. and myself

Dream 1, 16 June

I tell somebody word by word what the dancer told me yesterday: e.g., that she believed Minka was my mother. Mrs Lüchinger[89] replies: A little monkey that is brought here from his home's south.[ern] climate, gets a very different face (an unhappy sickly shrunken face, she says)

Explanation:
The dancer said e.g. that she took Minka for my mother.

Fr: People are extremely resourceful when they surrender to their unconscious.

(23)

Mrs Lüchinger replies: She is the only woman to put up a certain competition for her daughter.

Fr: So she relates to the manager of the boarding house—the mother in yesterday's dream—who was also a competition.

Addendum to yest.[erday's] dream: I use the lorgnette to look at the manager of the boarding house so as to annoy her. A clear motif of defiance. The little monkey: Minka, I thought, was quite nice back in her own country. Here in the foreign environment she derailed a.[nd] became sad. This morning France made plans what we could do, how we would live together in Siberia. I imagine Siberia to be very cold, so one could think of Switzerland as a southern home. "Then I'd be laughing on the other side of my face."

The little monkey also reminds me of the little monkey that was standing on Grandmama's writing desk. I was always asking: What does the little monkey think of me? Now it might be sad.

(24)

<u>Dream</u>: A terrible animal, a kind of beetle ~~with wings is~~ in the air and wants to bite me. It has the body of a shrimp and 2 horns like a snail. I think "stag beetle. As the stag panteth after water, so thirsts my soul after God."[90] I've never heard a stag pant for love X.[91] The animal flies like the firefly in the Chinese fairy tale, which was a god and flew into the woman's mouth and impregnated her.[92] It has 2 horns—castration. a crawfish's body—crabs move backwards—the member moves upwards, against gravity, thus against nature.

X Salts of hartshorn: laxative or emetic, thus an abort-inducing agent. Yesterday debate about abortion "Against nature" refers to this.

(25)

When I was 4 years old I called for Papa in the night [93]I felt something solid underneath me. He came, it was a lump of faeces. I was proud and not at all embarrassed, despite my age, which amazed me later. This gift was apparently a child.

Dream: I am sitting in a railway train and am traveling with Minka and a young man (France or Tag.[94][)] ~~He buys me~~ across the river Rhine into Germany. The landscape is inexpressibly beautiful, tall dark trees, everything has a distinct shine because it was raining, a peculiar shimmering rain. The young man buys me a newspaper, a kind of funny magazine, and a very silly one at that. A kind of illustrated story is in it: "How to hold off an ardent lover." Everything was idiotic. ~~One~~ It was a complicated procedure. One hands him something like a peashooter (Busch).[95] out of which comes fire. (In any case, he can no longer kiss.[)] In the dream, I am telling Freud about it, and when he

(26)

asks why I let him buy me the newspaper, I answer: I'm so just so dependent.

The dream ridicules Fr's advice, which is called idiotic. I am doing exactly the opposite, I am even going on my honeymoon with Fr, after all, the fact that Minka is present only proves it, so there are persons that represent the obstacle present in the dream to mask[96] what is going on. R. wanted to go to Germany with me for your honeymoon. This beautiful landscape with the fructifying rain is seen through t.[he] strange light of a passion.

F: You are under the rule of the defiance against t.[he] parents.

(He believes that this explains my love for the most part, but that's not true. Oh my God. How I love him.)

(27)

19th dream:

Fr. has stolen something, we are in the street and have to flee because of it. We want to take a tramway, but I say a car is better, it is faster. Then we are in a house and I want to put on other clothes, over or underneath the ones I'm wearing, so people won't recognise me. But as soon as I've done that, it is too hot, I cannot stand it.

*

A policeman is chasing us[97]

Notes

1. I thank Ulrike May for pointing out some of my transcription mistakes. AK.
2. Dividing line in original.
3. Double dividing line in original.
4. In the biblical narration, Adam fathers three sons after expulsion from the Garden of Eden: Cain, Abel, and Seth. In addition, the book Genesis (5:4) mentions further sons and daughters, who remain unnamed. "Adam Had Seven Sons", however, is a popular children's song.
5. Word is hardly legible; unclear reference.
6. Swiss German in the original ("The Hungerueli Isegrind devours his seven little children"). Hungerueli Isegrind is a fairytale figure from a Swiss nursery rhyme.
7. The reference most likely alludes to Schnitzler's novella *The Shepherd's Pipe* (1911).
8. Half a page is left empty here.
9. Here is an ink stain.
10. Abrupt "obstructions" were considered symptoms of schizophrenia. "Externally, 'thought-deprivation' is manifested in the form of 'obstructions'. The examiner suddenly receives no answer to his questions and the patient then states that he is unable to answer as his thoughts were 'taken away'." (Jung, 1907, p. 87).
11. A friend's name.
12. A friend's name.

13. *Psychanalyse* (instead of *Psychoanalyse*) in the original, which at the time was common terminology in Switzerland.
14. Translator's note: *gegen* ("against") in the original.
15. Translator's note: *es träumte mir* ("I was being dreamed") in the original.
16. "Everything, however, which appears conspicuously in the dream as a speech can be referred to real speeches which have been made or heard by the dreamer himself." (Freud, 1900a, p. 163).
17. After the ancient Greek city of Smyrna, located at the Gulf of Izmir. Smyrna carpets enjoyed great popularity in 19th century Europe.
18. Freud, 1905e.
19. Village in the canton Appenzell-Ausserrhoden, where the young Anna Guggenbühl stayed in a home for sick children. She had a delicate constitution, coughed a lot, and was prone to diseases of the lungs. The climate in Teufen was thought to alleviate such conditions.
20. That is, to the grandparents' house in this district, which was incorporated into Zurich in 1893.
21. Zurich street along the Sihl, in the vicinity of Bahnhofstrasse.
22. A recreational home that was built in Knollingen (Gufelstock), Engi GL municipality, where Anna Guggenbühl was sent during vacations when she was six or seven years old. Her two brothers also went. This home was also a convalescence facility for bronchitis and pneumonia patients.
23. Heavily crossed out. Word barely legible.
24. Faust I, Dungeon, Margaret:
    "If the mountain we had only passed!/There sits my mother upon a stone./I feel an icy shiver!/
    There sits my mother upon a stone,/And her head is wagging ever./ She beckons, she nods not, her heavy head falls o'er;/She slept so long that she wakes no more./She slept while we were caressing:/ Ah, those were the days of blessing!" (Lines 4564–4573, *Faust* by Johann Wolfgang Goethe, trans. Bayard Taylor, 2005–2014, Hazleton: Electronic Classics Series, http://www2.hn.psu.edu/faculty/jmanis/goethe/goethe-faust.pdf [last accessed 25 February 2015].
25. Translator's note: Swiss and Austrian term for high school diploma examination. *Matura* is also the general entrance qualification for university.
26. Tributary of the Rhine in Switzerland.
27. From this place to the next "Fr" ("You are free to insert the symbols yourself" etc.) runs a slightly wavy arrow on the left margin.
28. Here is a drawing of a symbol for femininity.
29. "[T]he sun […] is nothing but another sublimated symbol for the father." (Freud, 1911c).

30. Swiss carnival rhyme for the *Fasnacht*, when traditionally special *Fasnachtsküchlein* ("carnival pastries") are prepared.
31. Word is hardly legible.
32. Translator's note: *Wasserschmöcker* in original. Swiss German, literally translates as "water sniffers".
33. This topic concerned Freud a lot at the time. Two years earlier, he had published a paper discussing it (1919e); one of the presented cases seemed to connect to his daughter Anna (see Young-Bruehl, 1988), whose analysis (from October 1918 to the spring of 1922, with the second instalment between May 1924 and the summer of 1925; see Young-Bruehl, 1988 and Roazen, 1969) overlapped with the period when Freud was treating Anna Guggenbühl.
34. *par exemple* = for example.
35. The source for this parable could not be located.
36. See introduction.
37. Word is hardly legible.
38. Here follow three empty pages before the next entry.
39. Translator's note: *schön* ("beautiful") instead of the correct *schon* ("already") in the original.
40. In 1821, during a convalescent vacation at Marienbad, at 72 years of age, Goethe fell in love with Ulrike von Levetzow, who was only 17 at the time. Levetzow would turn down his proposal of marriage two years later. Goethe would channel the feeling of hurt upon this rejection in his *Marienbad Elegy*.
41. Word is hardly legible, and twice written over; the final result reads something like "Hannorrhihden".
42. That is, "He's a good person, but" etc.
43. Translator's note: *Abort* in the original, which in German can mean "toilet" and "abortion".
44. Translator's note: Freud here also uses the term *Abort*, see previous note.
45. Translator's note: *gegen* ("against") in original.
46. Translator's note: *schon* ("already") instead of the correct *schön* ("beautiful") in the original.
47. A lilac leaf signifies goodness deep within.
48. A fellow student.
49. Probably the Swiss psychiatrist Franz Riklin (1878–1938). Contributed studies to the Jungian association; first secretary of the International Psycho-Analytical Association) and, with Jung, editor of the *Korrespondenzblatt*. He followed Jung after the split from Freud. See Wieser, 2001, pp. 36 & 172–175. However, nothing is known about a possible connection between Anna Guggenbühl and Franz Riklin.

50. Some single letters are written here. They are barely legible and are crossed out.
51. Fellow student and lifelong friend.
52. Literally, a "treatment house", i.e. a hospital or nursing home.
53. *Hupel* ("bumpy") in original. However, the word is hardly legible; also possible: *Hugel* (perhaps misspelled for *Hügel*, little hill or bump).
54. A reference to Leo Tolstoy's novel *Resurrection* (1899).
55. Director at the Burghölzli, see introduction.
56. Word is a little hard to read.
57. Corrected (probably) over the letters "Bl".
58. Translator's note: *Mitesser* = blackheads. Literally, "fellow eaters", often with the connotation of parasites or freeloaders.
59. Closing quotation marks at this place in original.
60. Municipality in the Interlaken district, Canton of Bern.
61. The number "9" corrected over another number, probably "7".
62. Translator's note: *"Es schnitt mir furchtbar in die Seele"* (literally, "it cut deeply into my soul") in the original.
63. Written in the upper margin. The rest of the page is empty. Seven empty pages follow.
64. Written in the lower margin. The rest of the page is empty.
65. Translator's note: *Verstummelte* (word does not exist) instead of the correct *Verstümmelte* ("the maimed") in the original. *Stumm* = mute.
66. Word hardly legible.
67. *Doch* (= all the same), hardly legible; also possibly: *noch* ("still").
68. Cf. Freud, 1900a.
69. Translator's note: again, the incorrect *verstummelt* in original, see earlier note.
70. In front of this "d" is a doodle that looks like a smaller opening bracket.
71. Meaning unclear.
72. Refers to the so-called Venus de Milo, a statue on permanent display at the Louvre in Paris, where Anna Guggenbühl visited often.
73. Word is barely legible.
74. Reddish brown tuff, a porous, volcanic natural stone, was used by the Romans to build mansions and (thermal) baths.
75. Numerous lines at the bottom of the page are left empty.
76. A Vienna acquaintance.
77. Roughly translates as "dirty scoundrel"; derogatory term the French use for Germans.
78. One letter crossed out.
79. Name of a street in Zurich; Anna Guggenbühl's ancestral home.

80. In German, *du* ("you") is used as a form of address for friends, family, and associates, as opposed to the formal *sie* ("you").
81. Word is barely legible.
82. Translator's note: *es träumte mir* ("I was being dreamed") in the original.
83. *Schwabenkäfer* ("Swabian bug") in original = *Blatella germanica*, also known as German cockroach.
84. Title of a popular German Christmas song.
85. Translator's note: *Christkind* in the original. In German-language Christian mythology, the Christkind stands for Baby Jesus, but also—in its more commercially inclined incarnation—for the ghostly entity that puts the presents under the tree on Christmas Eve.
86. A boarding house with the address Hofzeile 29, in Vienna's 19th district (which is called Döbling). Other analysands of Freud also stayed there.
87. Person could not be identified.
88. Person could not be identified.
89. An acquaintance of Anna Guggenbühl's parents; her husband was a business associate of the father.
90. "As the hart panteth after the water brooks, so panteth my soul after thee, O God" (Psalm 42:1).
91. Reference to a footnote at the bottom of the page in the original.
92. The source of this fairy tale is unidentified.
93. One illegible mark at this place, probably an "f" crossed out.
94. Person not identified.
95. Possibly a reference to Wilhelm Busch's story *The Blowgun*. Anna Guggenbühl had studied German literature for a year before she turned to medicine, and knew Busch practically by heart. http://germanstories. vcu.edu/busch/puster_e.html [last accessed 26 February 2015].
96. Hardly legible; perhaps also: mark.
97. Here, in the centre of the page, the entries suddenly end.

Further reading

Cremerius, J. (1984). Freud bei der Arbeit über die Schulter geschaut. In: *Vom Handwerk des Psychoanalytikers: Das Werkzeug der psychoanalytischen Technik* (pp. 326–363). Stuttgart: Frommann-Holzboog.

Ferenczi, S., & Rank, O. (1924). *The Development of Psychoanalysis*. New York: Dover, 1956.

Freud, S. (1937d). Constructions in Analysis. *S. E.*, *23*: 257–270. London: Hogarth.

Freud, S., & Freud, A. (2006). *Briefwechsel 1904–1938*. Frankfurt: Fischer.

Freud, S., & Pfister, O. (1980). *Briefe 1909–1939*. Frankfurt: Fischer.

Jones, E. (1957). *The Life and Work of Sigmund Freud, Vol. 3*. New York: Basic.

Laplanche, J. (1998). Die Psychoanalyse als Anti-Hermeneutik. *Psyche*, 52(7): 605–618.

May, U. (2006). Freud's patient calendars: 17 analysts in analysis with Freud (1910–1920). *Psychoanalysis & History*, 9(2): 2007, 153–200.

Pohlen, M. (2006). *Freuds Analyse. Die Sitzungsprotokolle Ernst Blums*. Reinbeck: Rowohlt.

Roazen, P. (1995). *How Freud Worked*. Northvale, NJ: Aronson.

Sachs, E. (1913). Psychoanalyse oder Psychanalyse? *Internationale Zeitschrift für ärztliche Psychoanalyse, 1*: 100.

Wortis, J. (1954). *Fragments of an Analysis with Freud*. New York: Simon & Schuster.

References

Freud, S. (1900a). *The Interpretation of Dreams. S. E., 4–5*. London: Hogarth.

Freud, S. (1905e). Fragment of an Analysis of a Case of Hysteria. *S. E., 7*: 3–122. London: Hogarth.

Freud, S. (1911c). Psycho-Analytic Notes on an Autobiographical Account of a Case of Paranoia (Dementia Paranoides). *S. E., 12*: 3–82. London: Hogarth.

Freud, S. (1919e). *A Child is Being Beaten. S. E., 17*: 177–204. London: Hogarth.

Jung, C. G. (1907). *The Psychology of Dementia Praecox. Authorized Translation with an Introduction by Frederick Peterson and A. Brill*. New York: Journal of Nervous and Mental Diseases, 1909.

Roazen, P. (1969). *Brother Animal*. New Brunswick, NJ: Transaction, 1990.

Tolstoy, L. (1899). *Resurrection*. Oxford: Oxford University Press, 2009.

Wieser, A. (2001). *Zur früheren Psychoanalyse in Zürich 1900–1914*. Medical doctoral thesis, Zurich.

Young-Bruehl, E. (1988). *Anna Freud. A Biography*. New York: Summit, 1990.

CHAPTER TWO

Illustrations

This chapter offers a small collection of visual material relating to Anna Guggenbühl's life and diary. Illustrations 1a, 1b, and 1c are reproductions of the letter Freud sent to his future analysand: first, the envelope with Anna's address, and second, the pages in which Freud outlined his conditions for treatment with him. Illustration 2 shows Anna at 27, while in analysis with Freud. The following pages give insight into the diary proper: they reproduce the cover of the first notebook (Illustration 3), and some pages of her notes (Illustrations 4, 5, 6, 7, and 8). Illustration 9 features Anna at age three, which is also the time of her earliest memories. Next, some photographs of family and friends: a portrait of Anna with her parents and two younger brothers, Adolf and Walter, taken around 1900 (Illustration 10); a picture of Adolf and the sculptor Arnold H in Paris in 1920 (Illustration 11); one showing Anna in Paris in 1935, when her four children were already born (Illustration 12); and finally, the portraits of Adolf (Illustration 13), Anna's mother Anna Guggenbühl-Leuthold (Illustration 14), and Arnold H (Illustration 15), all taken in 1920 or 1921. Anna married the sculptor Arnold H in 1923 in Paris.

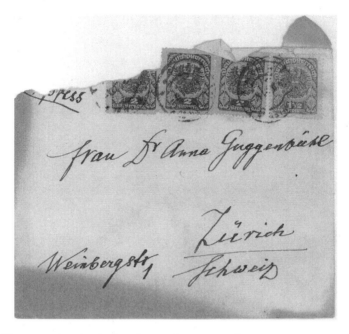

1a. The envelope of the letter from Freud to Anna Guggenbühl, March 1921.

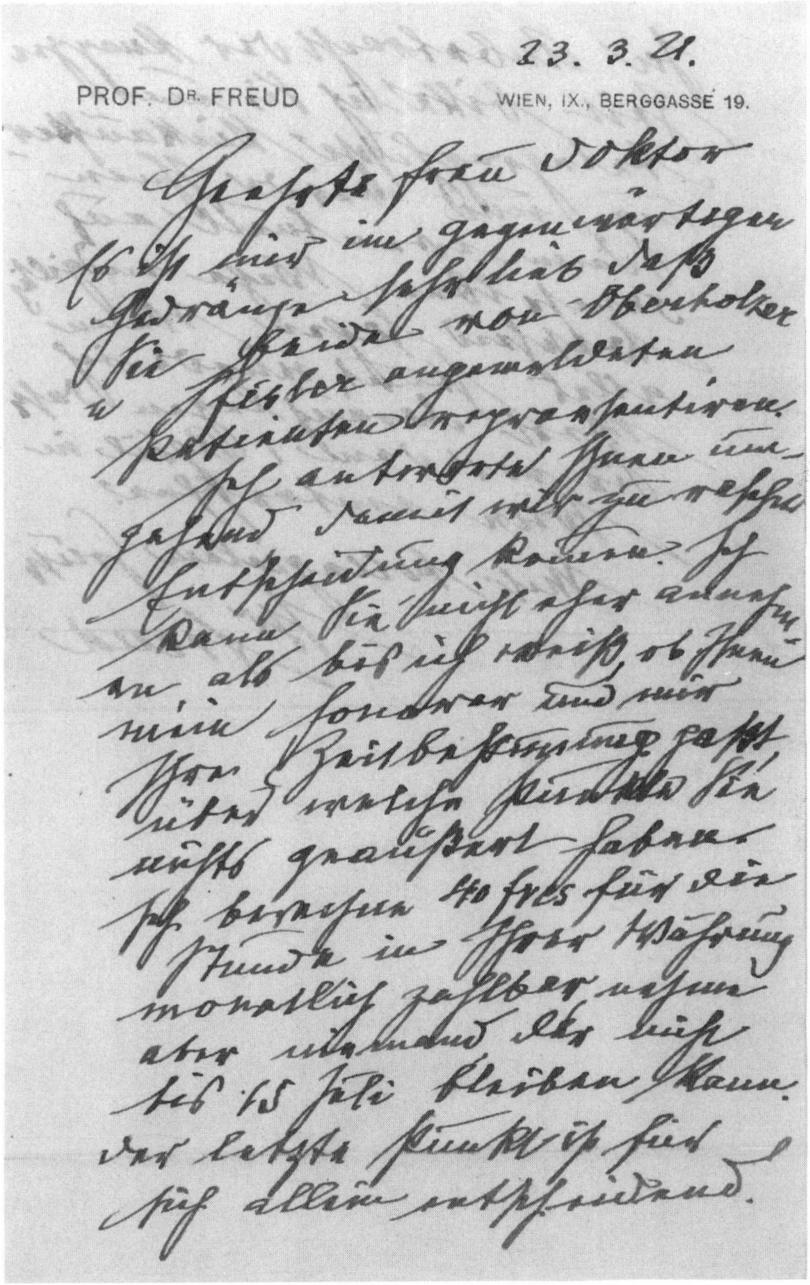

1b. Letter from Freud—page 1.

1c.   Letter from Freud—page 2.

2.   Anna Guggenbühl, in the year of her analysis with Freud in Vienna.

3.   Cover of the first diary.

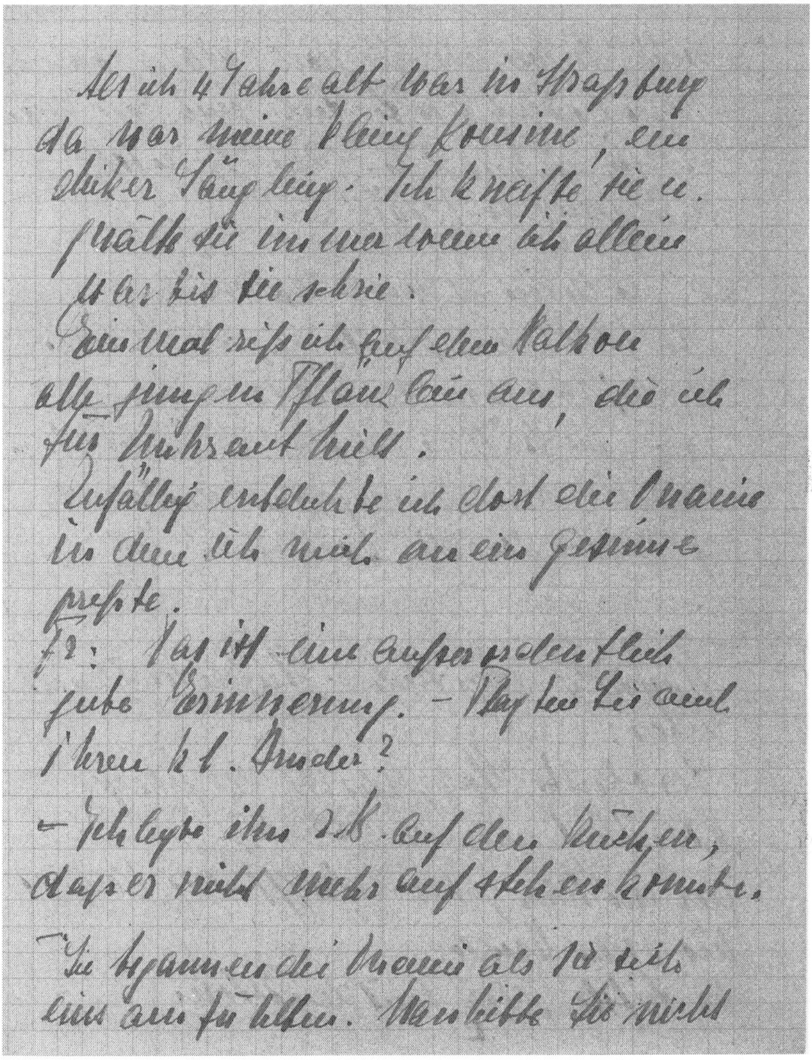

4. Diary I, page 1.

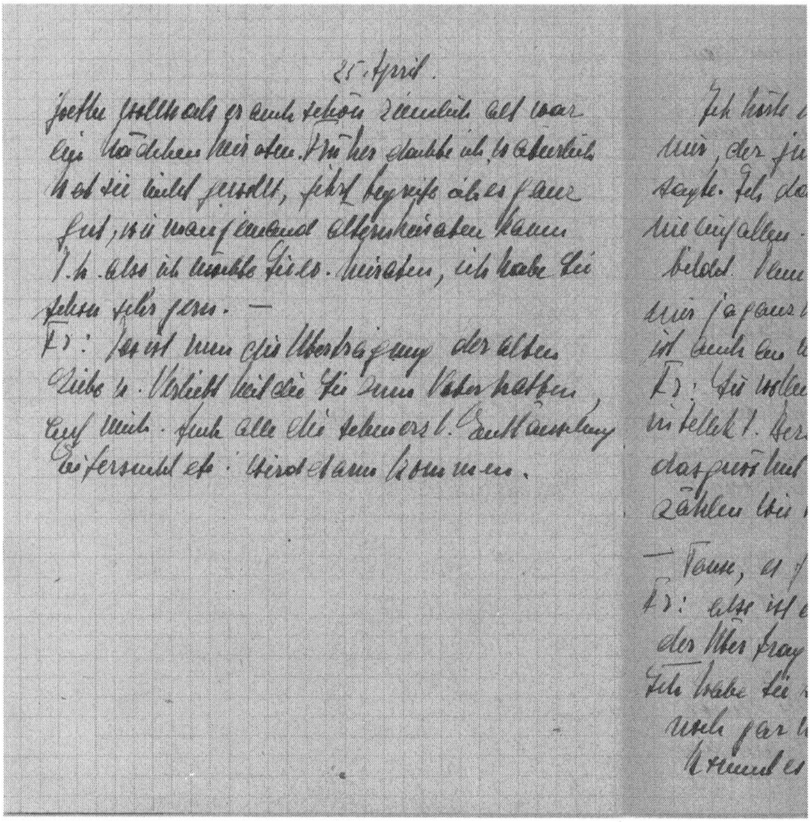

5. Diary I, page 31, Goethe.

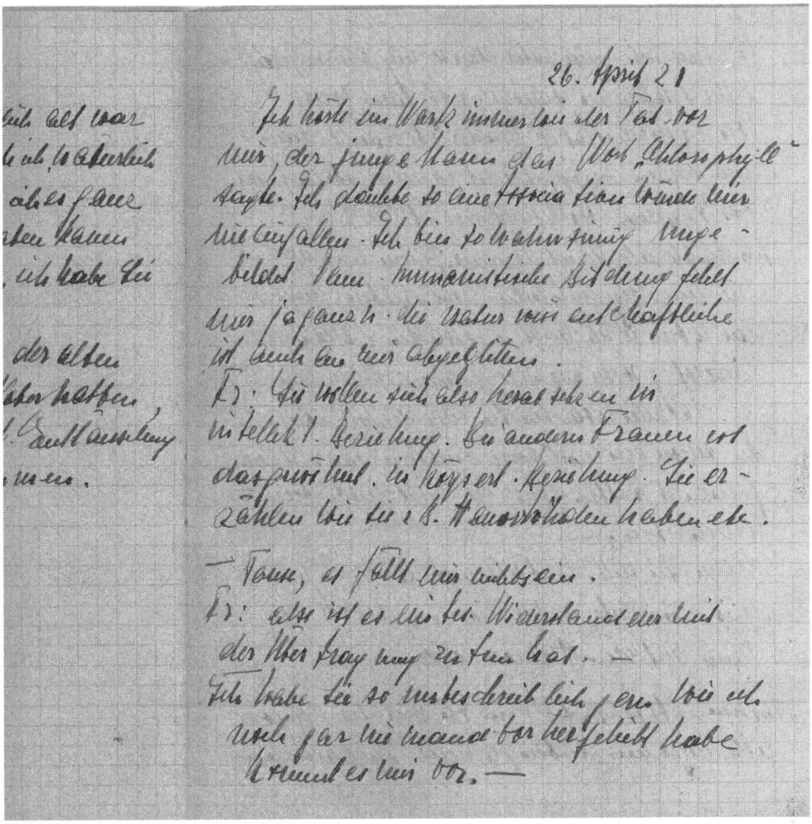

6. Diary 1, page 32, Chlorophyll.

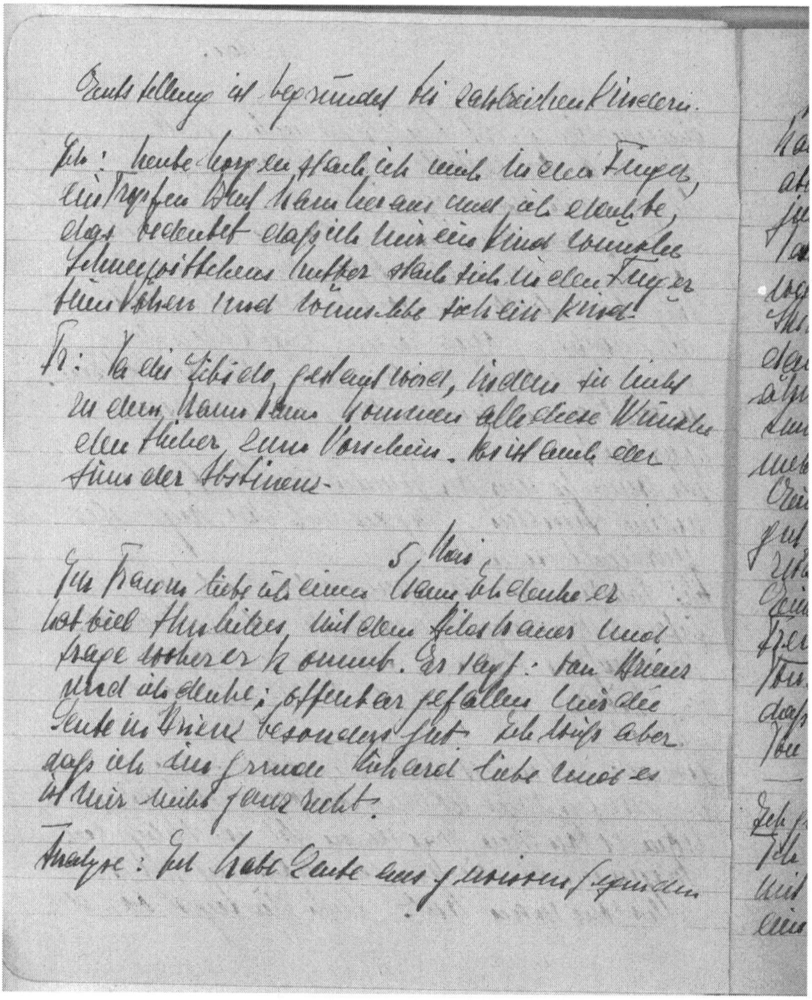

7. Diary II, page 2, sculptur.

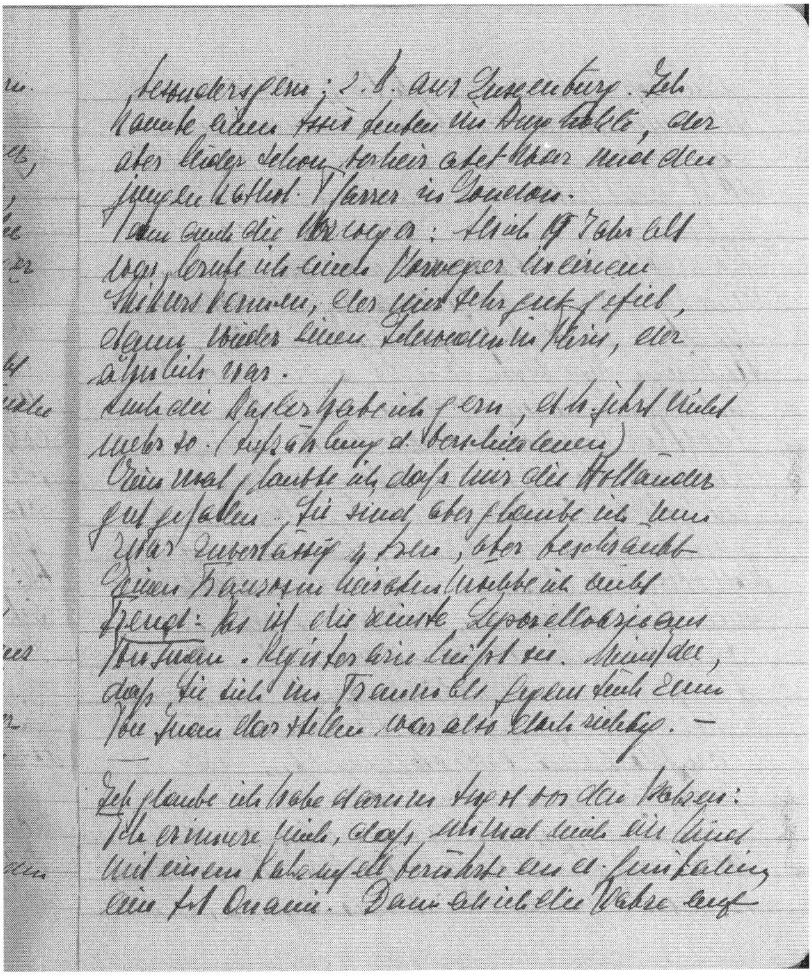

8. Diary II, page 3 Leporello.

9.   Anna, aged 3 years (1897), at the age of her first memories.

10. Anna, aged 6 years, with her parents and her brothers Adolf and Walter (1900).

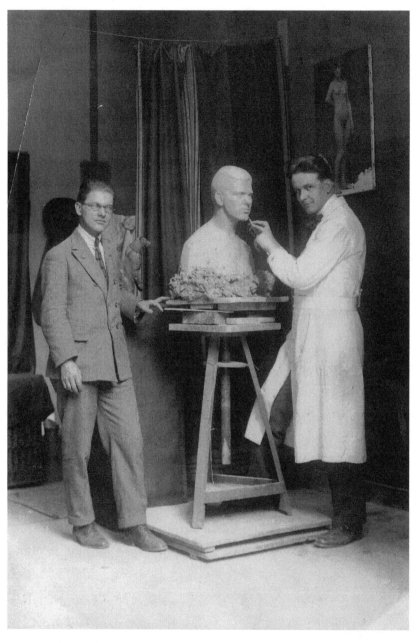

11.   Brother Adolf at the workshop of the sculptor, Arnold H, who
      married Anna in 1923 (Paris 1920).

12.   Anna in Paris (1935).

13.   Anna's brother Adolf.

14. Anna's mother.

15.   My grandfather, the sculptor.

CHAPTER THREE

Being analysed by Freud in 1921—notes about the analytic process*

Anna Koellreuter[†]

On 20 March 1921, Freud writes to Pfister:

Dear Dr. Pfister

I should of course be glad to accept a woman doctor for self-analysis, provided that she is prepared to pay the now usual forty francs an hour and remains long enough for there to be a prospect of getting somewhere, i.e. from four to six months; a shorter period is not worth while. I could certainly take her on October 1; whether I could take her earlier it is impossible to say. I am waiting to hear whether two patients due to begin on April 1 are really coming. You do not mention in your letter how much time the young woman is willing to devote to analysis. How her recent marriage will accord with an analysis lasting for many months I cannot say, so further information is desirable. (Freud & Pfister, 1963, pp. 81–82)

*Koellreuter, A. (2007). Being analysed by Freud in 1921—the diary of a patient. *Psycho-analysis and History Special Issue: Unknown Freud*, 9(2): 137–151.

[†]This chapter has been translated from the German by Ernst Falzeder.

The young doctor is my grandmother. As a matter of fact, she had not recently married but had been engaged to a fellow student for seven years. She was in analysis with Freud in Vienna from April to July 1921. In our family, we knew little about this analysis. She herself hardly talked about it. Why? This remains a secret that she took to the grave with her. I have been preoccupied by this fact all my life, particularly since I stayed with her in Zurich for a couple of years and had a close and warm relationship with her. We often talked about her work as a psychiatrist at the Burghölzli, the cantonal psychiatric university clinic there.

First, I would like to recount how I happened upon the diary. Second, I will present some biographical data about my grandmother. Third, I will say a few words about the format of the diary. There will then follow the main part of this chapter, namely, five extracts from the diary. Finally, I will present for discussion my thoughts on how Freud worked and, in particular, how he worked with transference.

My grandmother died in 1982 at the age of eighty-eight. Her claim that she had been in analysis with Freud sounded like an interesting but not quite realistic story to me. After her death, I sometimes found myself thinking: "Well, anybody could claim to have been in analysis with Freud ..." In 1989, my grandfather died at the age of ninety-five in Zurich, in the house in which he and his wife, together with their four children, had lived since 1939. It took months afterwards to empty out the house.

Then, one day, my mother called me on the phone, buzzing with excitement: "You know what I've found? The original letter from Freud to Grandma, in which he writes about the conditions for the analysis with him, dated 23 March 1921!" The letter reads as follows:

> Dear Doctor
>
> Given the present onrush [of patients] it suits me very much that you represent both of the patients promised by Oberholzer and Pfister. I am answering by return of post so that we can come to a quick decision. I cannot take you on before I know whether my fees are acceptable to you, and your schedule for me, about which you said nothing. I charge 40 francs[1] in your currency per hour, to be paid monthly, but cannot accept anybody who cannot stay until July 15. This last point alone is decisive. In view of the fact that time

is pressing, I ask you to answer by telegram, and will then let you know definitively, maybe in the same way.

If everything is in order, it is important that you arrive in Vienna before 1 April.

> With collegial regards,[2]
> *Freud*

Shortly afterwards, my mother called me again: "You'll never guess what I found this time! Two diary notebooks, like exercise books, in which Grandma wrote down things that happened during her analysis in Vienna!"

I took the books and read them in one go. For many years I was unable to deal with them in more depth, however, probably because of the intimate character of the notes, and put them aside for the time being. A few years later I picked them up again. I thought my resistances had subsided. Far from it! When I began to work with the diaries and to reflect on them, new resistances arose, which I found difficult to deal with. Many questions came to mind. What is a diary? Why does one write a diary? Did my grandmother write it for posterity? Or only for herself? And if she wrote it only for herself, why didn't she throw it away rather than keeping it? I kept a diary myself during my analysis, as did some of my colleagues to whom I talked. I used it as a means of sorting out certain things in my mind. After it had fulfilled its function I disposed of it. Was it because it had to do with Freud that my grandmother could not throw away her diary? Did she want to keep it as a historical document? I do not know. So I asked myself: Would she have wanted me to read the diary of her analysis? Would she have agreed to have parts of it published by me? Well, I suppose she would …

Biographical details

Anna Guggenbühl grew up in Zurich, together with her two younger brothers. One of them became a publisher, the other a painter. She herself at first studied German language and literature, and then—as one of only a few women at the time—medicine and psychiatry. When she started her analysis, she was 27 years old. She had already completed her medical studies, and had spent her first years of internship under Bleuler at the Burghölzli in Zurich.[3] As mentioned above, she had been engaged for many years, but the relationship with her fiancé had been quite ambivalent. The wedding had already been planned in great detail, and was supposed to take place in the autumn of 1921. My grandmother had ever-growing doubts about her future, however, but did not find the strength to disengage herself from this relationship, and this was precisely her reason for undergoing analysis. She often talked about this with me, but not about the analysis itself.

After Freud's letter arrived, it took her only two days to come to a definitive decision (the exact dates had only been settled by Freud's letter of March 23), namely, to go to Vienna and for four months to leave everything else to one side. When my mother cleared her parents' house, batches of letters were discovered, among them those that my grandmother had received during the months she had spent in Vienna. Most of them were from her father, a few from her mother, some from her fiancé, and finally two from my grandfather, whom she had got to know shortly before. It is evident from the content of these letters that she did not respond to them, or only very superficially, during those four months. We may speculate—but have no way of knowing—that Freud himself told her not to write back so as to ensure some "abstinence", in which she could come to a decision. Thus her father writes to her after a little more than two weeks: "Actually, I'm very angry with you, but this won't last, I can't help it. You should have written." And, at the end of the letter: "Pull yourself together now, including all your strength, pleasure, and also pain, write what you want to write, and whether Freud gives you *Freud*"[4] (17 April 1921). In a later letter he writes, with an ironic twist: "We have just received your letter that is so rich in content. Couldn't Freud cure you of your aversion to writing?" (18 May 1921) And, still later: "How is this Professor Freud, and how does he actually behave?" (13 June 1921).

The setting was as agreed upon in writing, and is in accordance with what Ulrike May (2006, 2007) and Christfried Tögel (2006) have discovered in their research into Freud's appointment calendars for the years between 1910 and 1920. The analysis began on Friday, 1 April 1921, and was conducted for one hour a day, six days a week, including Saturdays, as was the custom at the time. We know this from Freud's invoices, which were paid by her father.[5] The last analytic hour presumably took place on Thursday, 14 July, because on the next day, 15 July, Freud left for his holidays, and went to Badgastein with his sister-in-law (Jones, 1957, p. 79; cf. also Freud & A. Freud, 2006, p. 322). We recall that it was one of Freud's conditions that she remain until July 15. One last reference to my grandmother is found in Freud's letter to Pfister of 29 July 1921, from Badgastein (see below). We do not know whether she stayed on in Vienna afterwards, or if so, for how long. We may assume from one of the letters she received from her mother that the latter would have wished her to continue the analysis. Her mother wrote (17 June 1921):

> I also wondered if Prof. Freud couldn't give you an hour a day during the holidays, too. Such an interruption is really not good, especially as he himself emphasises in his book that there is something like a Sunday hour,[6] which has to be resolved on Monday. You could easily go to the same place where he spends his holidays, or what do you think about that? How long are Freud's holidays anyway? Six weeks? Or longer? It's all so difficult … You know, in his book Freud writes that there are patients who are treated for one year and longer.

The diary

I do not know what I expected or anticipated, but certainly not what I found, namely, a collection of scattered thoughts and statements in the form of a dialogue with Freud, in what seem to be direct quotes. She noted down what she found important, above all how Freud reacted to what she said. It is not possible to follow the analytic process in these hours.

This diary has a form different from others we know of. Ernst Blum's diary about his four-month analysis with Freud in 1922 (Pohlen, 2006) perhaps comes closest, but the two diaries and their backgrounds differ substantially. Blum saw himself as Freud's pupil and apprentice, on his way to becoming an analyst himself. My grandmother's goal in her analysis, however, was to get a clear idea of whether or not, after seven years of engagement, she really wanted that marriage to take place as planned in September 1921, as she told me several times. As we know from the letters, her parents never explicitly objected to breaking the engagement, but neither did they offer any help or advice. She told me that she was left alone with her problem, and also that breaking an engagement was quite something at the time. The notes in her diary are not well-rounded descriptions of the analytic hours, but apparently arbitrarily chosen thoughts or dream segments, which she probably wrote down after the hours. Nevertheless, we can obtain some information from them about Freud's way of working.

The diary consists of two exercise books in which she wrote her notes at irregular intervals. The first analytic hour took place on 1 April; however, her first entries are not dated, they are jotted-down notes that do not seem to reveal any structure of the hours. Only on page 7 do we find the first date: 15 April. The last entries in the second book are dated 16 June. In April she sometimes wrote daily, for May there are two entries, and four in June. The total number of sessions until the end of the analysis on 14 July 1921 is about eighty.

The first thing that catches the eye is how willingly, right from the beginning, my grandmother talked about sexual matters (as did Blum, by the way)—as if she wanted to present to Freud what he wanted to hear. Among the books she possessed there are most of Freud's psychoanalytic writings to 1920, as well as some by Rank, Stekel, Pfister, and the like. She had two copies of *Beyond the Pleasure Principle* (Freud, 1920g) and of *Three Essays on the Theory of Sexuality* (Freud, 1905d); both are so well thumbed that they nearly come apart. We may conclude that she studied parts of Freud's theory intensively, and that in all probability she had some knowledge of psychoanalysis when she began her analysis.

With regard to Freud's interpretations, three things in particular struck me in her notes. First, they are suggestive and leading; second, they are symbolistic; and third, they are reductive.

I will present five extracts and then add some remarks of my own.

First extract (pages 1–6, undated, i.e. at the beginning)

The very first entry reads:

G: When I was four years old, in Strasbourg, there was my little cousin, a fat baby. I pinched her, and when I was alone I always bullied her until she cried. Once I pulled out all the saplings on the balcony, I thought they were weeds. Incidentally, I discovered masturbation then, when I pressed myself against a cornice.

FR: This is a very remarkable memory. Did you also badger your little brother?

G: I turned him on his back, for instance, so that he could no longer get up.

FR: You started to masturbate when you felt lonely. You were no longer loved as much as you were as a single child. So you took revenge on the little child and on the symbol, the sapling.

G: When my brother W. was born, I asked when I saw him: Why doesn't he cry?

FR: So you would have liked to see him in a crying state, like your cousin?

FR: One can clearly see three levels in your life: the uppermost one is your present conflict with R., etc. The one in the middle concerns your relation to your brother. You are still quite unconscious of the deepest level, which is connected with your parents, and which is the most important one. It is from this that the relation to the brother is derived.

Later:

G: I tell Freud: When I went to the *Gymnasium*[7] I thought I would like to love a young man who was immensely sad, and I would make life possible for him, and then he would be happy.

FR: Like with your brother.

G: Then I thought that later I would like to have seven children; I did not think of the father.

FR: Seven men, actually. Seven?

G: Adam had seven sons. Papedöne[8] hangs his seven sons. The *Hungerueli* Isegrind devours his seven little children.[9] I believe male cats devour their offspring.

FR: You are coming so near the secret of the deepest level that I can break it to you: you loved your father and never forgave him his betrayal with the mother. You wanted to be the mother of the child. So you wished the mother, who took the lover away from you, dead. Bit by bit you will produce evidence for this, and the riddle of why you cannot get away from your brother will be solved.

Later:

FR: Three layers are easily recognisable in your life, the present one, which concerns the brothers, and the deepest one, which is connected with the parents. What is pathological is the long-lasting indecision whether or not you should marry R. The fact that no decision is reached proves that something else must lie behind it, something that is, as you recognise yourself, connected with the brothers and the parents.

G: In Paris, I liked W. [the one brother] so much; suddenly he, and no longer A. [the other brother], seemed to be my ideal.

FR: You glide from one to the other, just as you do with the lovers. The lovers are brother substitutes, that's why they are of the same age, actually younger in a social sense.

G: I'd like to go to Russia; like those aristocratic sons and daughters who left their families during the last revolution, I'd like to go away and leave the milieu in which I do not belong. I am thinking of that piece by Schnitzler, *Der Flötenton* [The sound of the flute].

FR: That is exactly your conflict.

Undated remark of Freud's (p. 11):

FR: Last time we saw that you are bored, that you would like to love somebody. Now there are two ways in analysis: some people have to do everything, the others, where enough mental material is present, deal with everything within their psyche. If possible, put a stop to the adventures. Bear it and suffer want, so that everything will come out all the more clearly in the analytic hour.

Second extract (p. 12, 18 April, "Dora")

G: Dream: "I was lying in bed in the evening, the light was on. Then I saw, on the left side of my head, disgusting, brownish stains on the sheet. Repellent little worms moved in the liquid (they [the stains] were still wet). I was disgusted and called my dad, and he was here and just laughed a bit, he was not frightened. It was like when I was a child and was scared, and he came." The Smyrna carpet in the oriel has brownish stains from the coffee that A. [the brother] and his friends drank there.

FR: So they are a bridge to the dream, to the brownish stains.

G: When I went to a café with the sculptor in my new dress, a young artist spilled coffee on my dress. I smiled and said: No problem. Once the sculptor embraced me. Afterwards there were stains on my dress, but it was a different dress. He was terribly sorry, but I said: No problem, really.

FR: So in the dream you call your father for help against the aggressions of the young men. You take refuge in your father. Your unconscious thus confirms my statement that your father was your first lover. Have you read the study on a hysteric, Dora?

G: Yes, but I don't remember anything.

FR: Your dream is completely modelled on Dora's one. So you take the place of Dora who, as we know, is in love with her father. At first there comes the intellectual willingness, then one accepts evidence from the unconscious, only then one admits it emotionally, and finally, as a conclusion, direct memories appear. Your love of the brother, conscious as it is, is not the deepest layer, and thus the knowledge of its existence is useless. You cannot free yourself from it because it has deeper roots.

Third extract (p. 21, 21 April, "The dream of the chessboard")

G: Friends of A. and W. [the two brothers] were there, but they were all a bit younger. They swam out into the lake, and the sun was shining. O. was there, and he was very little; I help him get over the wall because he couldn't do it on his own, and in the garden on the other side he suddenly threw himself on me and embraced me. I was a bit surprised that such a little boy dared do that, and I didn't really like it because there were people who were watching. Then I had a sweet little jewel case. I said, "The lid looks like a chessboard", but when I opened it, it was not like a chessboard at all. There were the loveliest things in it. For example, a little wedding party, little people cut out of paper so they could stand up. I wanted to give some to M. [the cousin], but I regretted it.

FR: The many friends …

G: They were all little, almost like children, O. in particular was very little. I helped him get over the wall, that is, I seduced him to love.

FR: Let us insert the symbols that we know thanks to our insights.

G: Chessboard: My father recently said he had played chess with my mother before they became engaged, and then he had asked her if she wanted to be his queen.

FR: You can insert the symbols also yourself, so that you can make a connection when you get stuck with the associations. Wall—this is the wall that has to be surmounted to embrace you. It is the hymen. The little jewel case is the female genital.

FR: The dream beautifully shows tendencies from the past. The box is like a chessboard, that is, you are taking the place of the mother, but afterwards: it is no chessboard after all, meaning, you turn away from the father. The friends, the "little ones", swimming around there, are symbols for the male member. You help him surmount the wall, that means, you want a real defloration that eventually leads to marriage (the little wedding party in the box). You begrudge your cousin M. the marriage. The sun is always the father.

Later:

G: Once, but only once, when Dad threatened to beat A. [the brother] as soon as we were home, I had a feeling of revulsion combined with some interest, but it was gone when the threat was put into action.

FR: This is the wish to be beaten yourself. Later on it takes the form of wishing to be merely scolded. When resistances arise in the analysis you behave in a similar way because I am representing the father; the idea that the cure is of no avail, for example, is already a beginning of that. Your anxiety that you might make an even more stupid choice in your marriage afterwards, because you wouldn't be able to endure it, is baseless, because the purpose of the cure is precisely to enable you to control that instinct and thus to be able to make a free choice of whom to marry, and not out of fear of the instinct. This objection is reminiscent of the story of the goose keeper and the horse keeper, who plan what they would do if they hit the jackpot. The horse keeper describes the palace in which he would live, the servants, etc. The goose keeper said he would just ride his horse and herd his geese. The idea that you would be too old to start a new life is all the more unjustified in that you prolonged your puberty to an extraordinary degree by your studies, and have had little experience.

Pause [sic].

G: At Burghölzli[10] there was a girl who was very intelligent and had a fine grasp of psycholog.[ical] understanding, she was called

Anna.[11] She wanted to ~~herself~~ learn stenography, but she did not get past the very first page, she could not focus at all.

G: I, too, cannot focus any more.
FR: Aha, a Swiss national diagnosis!

Fourth extract, part one (p. 34, 25 April, "erotic transference")

G: When Goethe was pretty old he wanted to marry a girl. In the past I thought that she, of course, did not like the idea, but now I see quite well that one might marry someone older. So this means that I might want to marry you; I really like you very much.
FR: Now this is the transference of the old love and infatuation you had for the father onto me. All the painful disappointments, the jealousy, etc., will come to light later, too.

Fourth extract, part two (p. 35, 26 April, "erotic transference")

G: In the waiting room I heard the patient who comes before me say the word "chlorophyll". I thought I could never come up with such an association. I am terribly ignorant. I lack all humanistic education, and I haven't absorbed scientific education either.
FR: So you want to belittle yourself intellectually. Other women usually do it in physical matters. They might say they've got haemorrhoids, etc.
G: (Pause) Nothing comes to mind.
FR: So this is a special resistance that has to do with the transference.
G: I can't tell you how much I like you; I think I've never loved anybody this way before.
FR: This love of the father was so enormous that everything that came later paled in comparison. People have no idea of the intensity of the love of children; it only exists in potential form, after all, and is not put into action.
G: When I was a child I always thought: let me never experience unhappy love, because my love is greater than that of other people.
FR: You are able to think all that only because you had already experienced disappointment at one time, which you did not remember

~~consciously~~. When you belittle yourself you do so to spoil your love for <u>me</u>, just like e.g. the lady with the haemorrhoids.

Fifth extract (p. 2/II, 5 May, "Leporello")

G: This morning I pricked my finger, there was a drop of blood, and I thought this meant that I wanted to have a child. Snow White's mother pricked her finger when sewing, and wished for a child.

F: Since the libido is dammed up because it cannot reach the man, all these wishes are surfacing here. This is also the purpose of abstinence.

G: In the dream I love a man. I think he bears many resemblances to the sculptor, and I ask him where he comes from. He says, from Brienz; and I think, obviously I have a particular fondness for people from Brienz. I know, however, that basically I am loving R. [the fiancé], and somehow this isn't right. I have a particular fondness for people from certain areas, from Luxembourg, for example. I knew an intern at the Burghölzli, but unfortunately he was already married, and there was the young Catholic priest in London. Then there are the Norwegians. When I was nineteen years old, I got to know a Norwegian at a skiing course, whom I found very attractive, then again a similarly attractive Swede in Paris. I also like men from Basle, actually no longer quite so (listing of the various men). Once I thought I liked the Dutch. But I think that, although they are reliable and faithful, they are quite limited. I wouldn't like to marry a Frenchman.

FR: This is quite a Leporello's aria, as in Don Juan. Catalogue Aria is what it's called. So my idea that in the dream you present yourself as a counterpart to Don Giovanni was right after all.

How Freud worked

Let me now add some reflections on how Freud worked. Regarding the question of suggestive and leading interpretations, Freud writes: "The danger of our leading a patient astray by suggestion, by persuading him to accept things which we ourselves believe but which he ought not to, has certainly been enormously exaggerated" (1937d, p. 262).

As far as his symbolic interpretations are concerned, he himself writes in *The Interpretation of Dreams*: "As a rule the technique of interpreting according to the dreamer's free associations leaves us in the lurch when we come to the symbolic elements in the dream-content." (Freud, 1900a, p. 353 [added 1914]) And he adds: "We are thus obliged, in dealing with those elements of the dream-content which must be recognised as symbolic, to adopt a combined technique, which on the one hand rests on the dreamer's associations and on the other hand fills the gaps from the interpreter's knowledge of symbols" (ibid.). For Freud, a knowledge of symbolism will "afford the most valuable assistance to interpretation precisely at points at which the dreamer's associations are insufficient or fail altogether" (Freud, 1901a, pp. 684–685 [added 1911]).

The diary notes show that Freud seems to have been quite generous with symbolic interpretations in this analysis. In *Psychoanalysis as anti-hermeneutics*, Laplanche discusses Freud's symbolism and states: "lorsque le symbolisme parle, les associations se taisent" [when symbolism speaks, the associations are silent] (Laplanche, 1999, p. 249).

Did Freud put a stop to the flow of associations by his symbolic interpretations, or did he, quite on the contrary, initiate them? Or did he get, by virtue of his suggestive aptitude, precisely those answers and associations that he wanted to get?

Finally, he reconstructively reduces expressions of transference nearly exclusively to the infantile-sexual level. We can also find such reductive interpretations of expressions of transference in other memoirs of his analysands, such as in those by Wortis (1954), Doolittle (1956), Blanton (1971), Dorsey (1976), Kardiner (1977), Blum (Pohlen, 2006) and others, as well as in Freud's technical writings (cf., Cremerius, 1984).

What interested me most in my grandmother's notes was the question: How did Freud *really* deal with transference in the analytic situation? Freud distinguishes between reconstruction and interpretation: "'Interpretation' applies to something that one does to some single element of the material, such as an association or a parapraxis. But it is a 'construction' when one lays before the subject of the analysis a piece of his early history that he has forgotten" (Freud, 1937d, p. 261).

In the work just quoted, Freud also raises the question of how one could verify whether or not a construction or reconstruction was correct. He discusses the meaning of the patient's acceptance or rejection of a reconstructive interpretation, and mentions the (unjust) "principle of 'heads I win, tails you lose'. That is to say, if the patient agrees with us, then the interpretation is right; but if he contradicts us, that is only a sign of his resistance, which again shows that we are right" (ibid., p. 257).

In their critical work *The Development of Psychoanalysis*, Ferenczi and Rank (1924) deal, among others, with this rather questionable position.[12] They write that in the past ten years Freud had not published any technical papers, and that this might be the reason why many analysts "adhered too rigidly to these technical rules" (ibid., p. 2). One might see the same danger in their own book, however, since Ferenczi and Rank put forward some technical rules themselves. They refer to Freud's paper "Remembering, Repeating and Working-Through" (Freud, 1914g), and hold that the wish to re-experience something— repetition or acting out—should not be considered as mere resistance, which would thus have to be avoided, but emphasise instead:

> From the standpoint of the compulsion to repeat, it is, however, not only absolutely unavoidable, that the patient should, during the cure, repeat a large part of his process of development, but also, as experience has shown, it is a matter of just those portions which cannot be really experienced from memory, so that there is no other way open to the patient than that of repeating, as well as no other means for the analyst to seize the essential unconscious material. (Ferenczi & Rank, 1924, p. 3)

Further on they add: "Thus we finally come to the point of attributing *the chief rôle in analytic technique to repetition instead of to remembering*" (ibid., p. 4, italics in original). Above all, they criticise that analytic therapy is hindered by previous knowledge of psychoanalysis, and that the main emphasis is put on remembering, while the affective component—experiencing—is neglected (cf., Turnheim, 1996, p. 87). They write: "An elimination, particularly of the intellectual resistances, is being increasingly required since psycho-analysis has begun to penetrate more generally into society, and people bring this knowledge as a means of resistance into the cure" (Ferenczi & Rank, 1924, p. 62).

They add that not only the analysand, but also the analyst, can have too much previous knowledge. It often happens, they continue, "that the associations of the patient were directed to the sexual factor at the wrong time, or that they remained stuck at this point if—as so often happens—he came to the analysis with the expectation that he must constantly talk exclusively of his actual or infantile sexual life" (ibid. p. 33).

Let us summarise. All this is about the "wish to re-experience" in the transference, which cannot always be dissolved and transformed into insight by interpretations. Consequently, there are "two kinds of knowledge" according to Ferenczi and Rank, "one intellectual, the other based on a deeper 'conviction'" (ibid. p. 45). It further follows that there is no analysis in which both analysand and analyst are not confronted with a residue that cannot be interpreted, a residue that neither of them is able to understand or dissolve by interpretations.

The way Ferenczi and Rank approach the problem of transference was of particular importance to me in discussing Freud's technique, as it becomes evident in these diary notes. What they miss in the then prevalent technique of interpretation is the importance, even crucial importance, played by "the analytic situation as such of the patient" (ibid., p. 30). The therapeutic effect, they argue, is only brought about by establishing the correct connection between the affect and the intellect. They stress the importance of realising the fundamental value of the transference in therapy, and they add that "*too much knowledge on the part of the patient should be replaced by more knowledge on the part of the analyst*" (ibid., p. 61, italics in original). That is to say that the analyst should set aside his knowledge, should make room for the libido in the analytic situation, and should tell the patient only what the latter "absolutely requires for the analytic experience, and its understanding" (ibid.). This additional knowledge includes the fact that the analyst knows that he knows nothing—he does not know how the analysand coped with his traumatic experiences. This seems to point in the same direction as Lacan's "sujet supposé savoir" (the subject who is presumed to know). Laplanche calls this the "transfert en creux", the "hollowed-out" or "empty" transference, in which there is nothing to interpret (Laplanche, 1987, pp. 156–158). This hollowed-out transference represents the space in which interpretations of all kinds are possible. This also means that, when this space is missing, transference interpretations must fall on infertile ground. There will always remain a residue in this room, a residue which is not understood by either side, and which therefore cannot be interpreted. What can we say about Freud's technique of dealing with transference in these notes? It is well known that Freud explained transference in a reductive way, tracing it back to infantile sexuality or the infantile affect, which would then be repeated in the analytic situation. He paid relatively little attention to the analytic situation itself, that is, to what actually happened between himself and the analysand (Cremerius, 1984, p. 342). This is also described in Blum's diary: "Detaching myself from Freud never posed any difficulties, since during the whole analysis Freud never 'offered' himself as a transference object, but as a reliable analytic dialogue partner, who allowed for open equality with him" (Pohlen, 2006, p. 283). Cremerius remarks that Freud did not follow up certain transferential offers, as in the case of the "Rat Man", who had told him at the beginning of the hour that he was hungry (Cremerius, 1984, p. 343). By and large, this is also the way in which he worked in the analysis of my grandmother. There is one passage in the notes, however, where Freud—in a rather surly manner, perhaps—interprets the psychoanalytic situation: "When you belittle yourself you do it to spoil your love for *me*, just like the lady with the haemorrhoids."

Nevertheless, one can state that Freud did offer himself as a transference object in the case of my grandmother, too. Roazen quotes Freud's analysand Hirst as saying "that the mere fact that he was talking to Freud had more of a therapeutic effect than anything that Freud had said to him" (Roazen, 1995, pp. 27–28). My mother remembers a remark of my grandmother that it was Freud's presence, his being in the same room, above all, that had been effective; words were only of secondary importance.

He was suggestive and seductive, and partly also very active, but at the same time he kept his distance in the analysis, as he did in most cases.[13] Thus he was able, without actually dealing with the present transference situation, to create a transferential space—the "hollowed-out transference", in Laplanche's term—in which he could interpret, in a reductive way, the sexual-infantile transference—in the "filled-in transference", "le transfert en plein", as Laplanche calls it.

To conclude, I would like to quote from a hitherto unpublished letter of Freud's to Pfister, in which he mentions the end of my grandmother's analysis.[14] It was written in Badgastein on 29 July 1921, two weeks after the analysis had ended: "The little G. became totally transparent, and she is actually finished—but what life will now do to her I cannot know." Engrossed in my wishful thinking I produced a veritable parapraxis, and proudly said to myself: My grandmother understood what it was all about! She saw through it all! But then Ulrike May pointed out to me that Freud often made similar statements in his correspondence, and that this meant no more than Freud himself understood—or thought he understood—what it was all about, but that he could not tell if she herself had understood "it". So, what did life do to her? Upon her return from Vienna, she packed her bags in Zurich, called off the wedding, which had been planned for September, and immediately took off for Paris to join her brother. There she took up a position in a psychiatric clinic, and soon fell in love with my grandfather—the sculptor from Brienz—who happened to be in Paris at the same time. They married in 1923, had four children, lived in Paris until the outbreak of war in 1939, and then moved on to Zurich. They stayed together for 60 years until her death.

There is one question I have not been able to answer to the present day. Why did she not become an analyst herself?

Notes

1. The fee of 40 Swiss francs was, in April 1921, equivalent to £1.15 or US$ 6.90 (Ed.).
2. Translator's note: in the original, "Mit kollegialen Grüßen", a common salutation among doctors at the time. As with so many other salutations, there is no exact equivalent in English. I have chosen to translate it literally for two reasons: first, this formula was extremely rarely used by Freud in his later years; second, I find it noteworthy that he did use it in his letter to this young female doctor, who had just completed her training.
3. She took up her first post there after the Staatsexamen (final examination) in 1918. In 1920, she also wrote her medical dissertation under Bleuler at the Burghölzli.
4. Translator's note: untranslatable play on the word "Freud(e)" = joy, pleasure.
5. Two monthly money transfers are extant.
6. Translator's note: in the original: "Sonntagsstunde"—obviously a mistake for "Montagskruste" = Monday crust. "Even short interruptions have a slightly obscuring effect on the work. We used to speak jokingly of the 'Monday crust' when we began work again after the rest on Sunday" (Freud, 1913c, p. 127).
7. Translator's note: the equivalent of grammar or high school.
8. Translator's note: "P." in the original.

9. Translator's note: in the original this sentence is written in Swiss German; the Hungerueli Isegrind is a fairy-tale figure.
10. See introduction.
11. Word is hardly legible.
12. In this context, I cannot enter into a discussion of this book's role in the history of the "Secret Committee", to the eventual dissolution of which it contributed.
13. An exception is the analysis of Wortis (1954), who could not wait until the analysis ended.
14. My thanks go to Ernst Falzeder who made this letter (Freud Collection, Library of Congress) available to me.

References

Blanton, S. (1971). *Diary of My Analysis with Sigmund Freud*. New York: Hawthorn.

Cremerius, J. (1984). Freud bei der Arbeit über die Schulter geschaut—Seine Technik im Spiegel von Schülern und Patienten. In: *Vom Handwerk des Psychoanalytikers: Das Werkzeug der psychoanalytischen Technik* (pp. 326–363). Stuttgart: frommann-holzboog.

Doolittle, H. (1956). *Tribute to Freud*. New York: Norman Holmes Pearson.

Dorsey, J. M. (1976). *An American Psychiatrist in Vienna*, 1935–1937, and his Sigmund Freud. Detroit, MI: Center for Health Education.

Ferenczi, S., & Rank, O. (1924). *The Development of Psychoanalysis*. New York: Dover, 1956.

Freud, S. (1900a). *The Interpretation of Dreams*. S. E., 4–5. London: Hogarth.

Freud, S. (1901a). *On Dreams*. S. E., 5: 633–686. London: Hogarth.

Freud, S. (1905d). *Three Essays on the Theory of Sexuality*. S. E., 7: 130–243. London: Hogarth.

Freud, S. (1913c). On Beginning the Treatment: (Further Recommendations on the Technique of Psycho-Analysis I). S. E., 12: 123. London: Hogarth.

Freud, S. (1914g). Remembering, Repeating and Working-Through: (Further Recommendations on the Technique of Psycho-Analysis, II). S. E., 12: 147–156. London: Hogarth.

Freud, S. (1920g). *Beyond the Pleasure Principle*. S. E., 18: 7–64. London: Hogarth.

Freud, S. (1937d). Constructions in analysis. S. E., 23: 257–269. London: Hogarth.

Freud, S., & Freud, A. (2006). *Briefwechsel 1904–1938*. Frankfurt: Fischer.

Freud, S., & Pfister, O. (1963). Psychoanalysis and Faith. The Letters of Sigmund Freud and Oskar Pfister. New York: Basic.

Jones, E. (1957). *The Life and Work of Sigmund Freud, Vol. 3*. New York: Basic.

Kardiner, A. (1977). *My Analysis with Freud: Reminiscences.* New York: Norton.

Laplanche, J. (1987). *Nouveaux fondements pour la psychanalyse.* Paris: Presses Universitaires de France. D. Macey (Trans.) *New Foundations for Psychoanalysis.* Oxford: Blackwell, 1989.

Laplanche, J. (1999). La psychanalyse comme anti-herméneutique [1995], in *Entre séduction et inspiration: L'homme.* Paris: Presses Universitaires de France. Psychoanalysis as anti-hermeneutics. *Radical Philosophy, 79*: 7–22, 1996.

May, U. (2006). Freuds Patientenkalender: Siebzehn Analytiker in Analyse bei Freud (1910–1920). *Luzifer Amor: Zeitschrift zur Geschichte der Psychoanalyse, 14*(37): 43–97.

May, U. (2007). Neunzehn Patienten in Analyse bei Freud (1910–1920): Zur Dauer von Freuds Analysen (Teil I) Zur Frequenz von Freuds Analysen und weiteren Beobachtungen (Teil II). *Psyche: Zeitschrift für Psychoanalyse und ihre Anwendungen 61*: 590–625, 686–709.

Pohlen, M. (2006). *Freuds Analyse: Die Sitzungsprotokolle Ernst Blums.* Reinbek bei Hamburg: Rowohlt.

Roazen, P. (1995). *How Freud Worked.* Northvale, NJ: Aronson.

Tögel, C. (2006). Sigmund Freuds Praxis.Visiten und Ordination—Psychoanalysen—Einnahmen. *Psyche: Zeitschrift für Psychoanalyse und ihre Anwendungen, 60*: 860–880.

Turnheim, M. (1996). Nachwort. In: S. Ferenczi & O. Rank, *Entwicklungsziele der Psychoanalyse: Zur Wechselbeziehung von Theorie und Praxis* (pp. 85–95). Vienna: Turia + Kant.

Wortis, J. (1954). *Fragments of an Analysis with Freud.* New York: Simon & Schuster.

CHAPTER FOUR

"Prof. Freud calls for tolerance!"— Dashes that moved the couch and politics*

Karl Fallend

T he advancement of psychoanalysis virtually came to a halt during the First World War. Many analysts were drafted, or unavailable because they resided in what now counted as enemy territory. Severe material dearth impeded intellectual exchange and academically productive work. Toward the end of the war, however, psychoanalysis seemed to have established itself in society to a surprising degree: after all, its methods had proven more effective in the treatment of war neuroses than those of classical psychiatry. As a consequence, military administrations in Germany, Hungary, and Austria "seriously considered opening their own psychoanalytic wards within their armies, a project that was interrupted only by the eventual end of the war ... In any case, the experiences during wartime promoted the dissemination of an interest in psychoanalysis throughout the world."[1] While psychoanalysts were spared engagement under the patronage of the military, the newly acquired worldwide interest changed the future

*Time and again, and this time in particular, I would like to thank my partner Gabriella Hauch for her feminist critique and her support.

of psychoanalysis. The former small circle of quirky scientists grew into an international movement.

In the year 1921 alone, interested parties inquired about psychoanalysis from South Africa, Australia, Bulgaria, Brazil, and India. By 1922, the meetings of the Vienna Psychoanalytic Society drew so many foreign visitors that on 13 June, its members had to vote on a revised guest policy. This post-war development of psychoanalysis became the most rapid in its history. Anton von Freund, a wealthy Hungarian industrialist, donated part of his estate to the psychoanalytic movement, which allowed Freud to make his pet project, the foundation of a psychoanalytic press, a reality in 1921. The Viennese communal elections of 4 May 1919, in which the Social Democrats won an absolute majority, marked the beginning of *Austromarxismus*, the socio-political project that gained international recognition especially for its impressive "Red Vienna" social housing projects. Social Democrat councillor Julius Tandler launched a comprehensive reform of public health and welfare services, which resulted in the establishment of marriage guidance bureaus, school dental clinics, welfare centres for alcoholics, clinics for sufferers of venereal diseases, and so on in Vienna. By 1920, the city's psychoanalysts joined in the reforms. Following the example of their Berlin colleagues, they began planning a psychoanalytic outpatient clinic, to open in 1922. A new professional profile of the "psychoanalyst" emerged. Questions of training were posed with a new urgency: who was allowed to call themselves a psychoanalyst? What should be the criteria when choosing new members? Possible steps to institutionalisation were discussed intensively, for instance at the International Psychoanalytic Congress in Den Haag in 1920. The triad of internationalisation, institutionalisation, and professionalisation marked the psychoanalysts' hungry dedication after the barren war years. Their commitment seemed to defiantly counter the highly volatile social, economic, and political conditions they were working in, which were, after all, dominated by a fear of chaos and anarchy.

When Anna Guggenbühl arrived in Vienna in March 1921, she could probably guess from her own experience in Zurich what awaited her in the metropolis of the fallen Habsburg monarchy. In November 1917, infuriated mass demonstrations in Zurich had demanded the release of the incarcerated pacifist Max Dätwyler. The protest was violently crushed by the police, which resulted in several fatalities on the protestors' side (see Teslin, 1919, pp. 1–26). Though neutral during the war,

Switzerland nevertheless had to alleviate hunger and deal with food shortages in public soup kitchens. As a result of the growing frustration, Zurich residents had joined the national strikes of October 1918 and November 1919, which were quelled by the army after a few days. In 1919, the Social Democrats had become the second strongest party in the Swiss national council. Anna Guggenbühl had witnessed the masses on the streets. What she had seen were revolutionary offshoots spreading from Russia throughout Europe. In Austria, now merely a federal state, these offshoots met with a particularly strong empathic response.

The successful Russian revolution of 1917 had inspired insurrections in Munich, Bremen, and Berlin. The Spartacist uprising was brutally put down, its leaders Karl Liebknecht and Rosa Luxemburg arrested and executed. In Budapest, revolutionaries led by Béla Kun created the Party of Communists from Hungary and installed a short-lived government run by socialists and communists. The Habsburg monarchy lay in ruins. After exercising power for more than six decades, Franz Josef, once a symbol of fatherly stability, was history, leaving a palpable vacancy.

In many aspects, the almost bankrupt Austria resembled what we might today call a developing country. Hunger, tuberculosis, and other epidemics raged. Many homes could not be heated for lack of coal. Compared to 1914, the expense of living had multiplied by 150, while incomes had only grown by a factor of forty. The central bank could hardly issue enough notes, and the formerly powerful Vienna bourgeoisie was forced to sell jewellery and paintings in order to survive (Pfoser, Pfoser-Schewig, & Renner, 1993, p. 82ff). Sigmund Freud, too, had lost his savings. Only by treating foreign patients could he support himself and start saving again. In particular, income from American colleagues like Horace Frink and Monroe Meyer significantly contributed to the fact that Freud—as Otto Rank puts it in a letter to the committee on 1 March 1921—"had at least won back a third of his pre-war estate" by the early 1920s.[2]

After *The Last Days of Mankind* (the title of Karl Kraus's 1919 epic, satirical play about the First World War), the masses who had lost the war suffered from poverty, starvation, and the insecurity of what power would take the place vacated by the monarchy, which had, after all, ruled for centuries. Not many thought that the small Austrian state would be able to survive. In referendums in the Tyrol (April 1921) and

Salzburg (May 1921),[3] more than ninety per cent voted to annex Austria into Germany.

Which World? asked Hauch (2008). In the years after the First World War, that was the central question the population set out to answer by mass strikes, mass demonstrations, and mass movements—social phenomena whose momentum, frequency, and aggression not only caused excitement and hope but also, for many, upset and anxiety, and which Freud and his followers reflected in their psychoanalytical methods.

Right after the war, at the peak of the social revolutionary phase, Paul Federn was first to enter the public arena with a psychological analysis of the *Räte*—the workers' councils. His analysis, published in *Österreichischer Volkswirt* in March 1919, was titled "Towards a psychology of the revolution. The fatherless society". To Federn, father–child relations constituted the affective basis for every authoritative relationship, which he saw reflected in an overly visible manner in the political organisations of his day. The yearning for fatherly security, power, might, and protection affects the choice of father figures after the fall of the actual father. Federn located the potential for change in the new organisational form of the *Räte*, which had risen and received its impulses from the grassroots, and whose unconscious psychological system constituted a fraternal relationship. The actual psychological problem in Federn's view was the formation of a non-patriarchal social order (1919, p. 76). Still, Federn was aware of the tenacious effects history can have. He expressed this awareness with the simple observation of an older comrade who, while fluently and confidently rallying for the most radical beliefs, stumbled more than twenty times over the few sentences that demanded the emperor's abdication. "Within him, the child who is loyal to the Emperor has left the social democratic man—as the popular saying goes—speechless"[4] (ibid., p. 72). Paul Federn, himself an active social democrat, considered the Social Democrats chastened, as its founder Victor Adler provided the sort of leader to whom party members could satisfyingly direct their ideational need for a father figure. Adler's son Fritz was seen by the party as a heroic figure, and his assassination of Prime Minister Count Stürgkh was viewed as an act of vehement opposition against the old authoritarian state (ibid., p. 75).

As Federn's analysis of the revolution was published, Freud himself seemed to have already entertained thoughts of subjecting the psychological phenomenon of the ideological group to an analytical investigation. On 12 May 1919, he wrote to his friend Sándor Ferenczi that he had just "attempted a psychoanalytical foundation for group psychology with a very simple idea" (Jones, 1962, p. 59). Though often interrupted—after all, Freud was engaged with *Beyond the Pleasure Principle* at the same time—the work on this idea would eventually grow into a book, *Group Psychology and the Analysis of the Ego* (1921c). This book was finally published in August 1921,[5] which means that Freud was working on it during Anna Guggenbühl's analysis. Freud opens his explication with a radical critique of a binary conception of the individual and the group: "The contrast between individual psychology and social or group psychology, which at a first glance seems to be full of significance, loses a great deal of its sharpness when it is examined more closely ... [s]o from the very first individual psychology ... is at the same time social psychology as well" (Freud, 1921c, p. 3). He elaborates that erotic relations, in the form of *zielgehemmte* (aim-inhibited) libido, connect the members of a group horizontally, but also vertically. By using the example of two "artificial groups", the church and the army,[6] Freud analyses the psychodynamics of a "suggestion of an illusion", that is, the idea that a leader loves everybody equally and justly. On the one hand, each individual is libidinally bound to the leader—Christ or the General—and on the other hand, to the other individuals in the group. According to Freud, the impending disintegration of this erotic relation results in "social anxiety", an aimless fear and panic that analogously manifests in the individual's neurotic anxiety at the breakup of emotional attachments. This fear necessitates defences, which in turn contribute to a strengthening of the bond, and cause the individual to direct their hostile impulses to the outside: "Therefore a religion, even if it calls itself a religion of love, must be hard and unloving to those who do not belong to it" (ibid., p. 36). Here, Freud emerges as a fundamental critic of religion, which, given the Stalinist development of Russia, bears political–prophetic potential, as he continues:

> Fundamentally indeed every religion is in this same way a religion of love for all those whom it embraces, while cruelty and intolerance towards those who do not belong to it are natural to every religion ... If today that intolerance no longer shows itself so violent and cruel as in former centuries, we can scarcely conclude that there has been a softening in human manners. The cause is rather to be found in the undeniable weakening of religious feelings and the libidinal ties that depend upon them. If another

group tie takes the place of the religious one—and the socialist tie seems to be succeeding in doing so—then there will be the same intolerance towards outsiders as in the age of the Wars of Religion. (ibid., p. 36)

Freud's reflections on "group psychology" were timely, as he focused on psychogenic phenomena and processes that he could observe in great numbers in the contemporary changes manifesting in everyday political life. The growth of political parties into mass organisations and the public display of so many different ideologically motivated groups, across national borders and to such great extent, were new social phenomena. Freud, like most of his colleagues, had already passed his prime, his ideas firmly a part of *The World of Yesterday* (Zweig, 1944). The appearance of young students—especially young female students—in the Vienna Psychoanalytic Society's regular discussion panels did not only signify a generational break, but also the advent of new ideas that would radically alter the world. These ideas were formulated by voices that had been denied the right to be heard for centuries: those of young people and of women. The analogies in the suppression of these two groups had already been detected in 1914 (cf., Fallend, 1992), with Siegfried Bernfeld, leader of the radical Vienna Youth Movement and future psychoanalyst, remarking in a brochure that "the ideas of the new youth and those of the modern women correspond to and necessitate each other" (Bernfeld, 1914, p. 37). This new, predominately urban avant-garde postulated the ideals of freedom, emancipation, and autonomy in all spheres of life, and measured the new democratic republic against their demands. Freud and his colleagues were confronted with the same claims and ideals. On 2 June 1920, barely a year before Anna Guggenbühl began her analysis with Freud, Otto Fenichel, a medical student and cohort of Bernfeld, addressed the Vienna Psychoanalytic Society with a talk titled "Sexual questions in the youth movement". In the following discussion, Freud appeared slightly perplexed and not entirely sympathetic, but nevertheless reacted with openness and tolerance. "Prof. Freud feels quite removed from the problems of these times. Thinks that in the present order of society not to help.[7] Abstinence, but under protest! Calls for tolerance!" And the minutes continue: "Effects of ascesis of the youth: creates vigorous men, effects show as deformity of character, not as neuroses, e.g. Switzerland. Is the consequence of strong restriction of the sexual" (Fallend, 1995, p. 200f).

These stereotypical remarks are hard to pin down. However, they may have resulted from Freud's experience of a repressive "civilised sexual morality" that shortly afterwards he would also encounter in exchanges with his Swiss psychoanalyst colleagues.

Georg Groddeck, the physician, social reformer, and writer from Baden-Baden, was one of the "misfits, dreamers, sensitives" (A. Freud, 1968, p. 2,489) among psychoanalysts to whom Freud felt most empathically inclined. With his psychoanalytic novel *The Seeker of Souls*, Groddeck caused a veritable stir. The novel was published in early 1921 by the Internationaler Psychoanalytischer Verlag, and met Freud's sensibilities spot on in passages like the following, in which the author has his protagonist Thomas Weltlein exclaim: "Behold, how great the earth is and how small the little things that strike you as so important; look around you, the small pleasures that sexuality shall bring, you shall find them everywhere. The world is awash with them." The prudery of his colleagues, who were enraged about the book lest it should damage the image of the psychoanalytic profession, amused Freud. On 23 January 1921, Freud wrote to Max Eitingon: "I am quite entertained by the collective frowns that Groddeck's novel arouses in analysts even within our close circle. With the hypocrite Swiss or the anagoge[8] Silberer there I don't wonder, but otherwise I cannot but observe that it is a treat, caviar for the masses, of course, but nevertheless the work of a mind equal to that of Rabelais."[9]

Such praise was not trivial—neither were the reasons that quickly transformed Freud's initial amusement into irritation. After a protest meeting held by the Swiss Psycho-Analytical Society, the Psychoanalytic Press in Vienna received a harsh letter, hitherto unmatched in the history of psychoanalysis. For the first time, a local chapter, eager to show compliance before there was even a charge, spoke out in favour of censoring a psychoanalytic publication, and demanded that the publisher prohibit distribution of Groddeck's *The Seeker of Souls*. This went too far. On 28 February 1921, Freud and Otto Rank prepared on behalf of the executive board of the Psychoanalytic Press, an unambiguous ten-page statement that did not invite further debate. Among other things, the document clearly stated that Freud and Rank would sincerely regret having "to conclude that our Swiss colleagues accepted our psychoanalysis only to arrange, in solemn silence, a first-class funeral of its sexual content, and we hope that this is not the case."[10]

What was at stake in this debate was not ethical issues, or matters of literary taste. The Swiss colleagues had shaken the very foundations of psychoanalysis. It seems not unreasonable to assume that Anna Guggenbühl—Freud's famous name notwithstanding—also went to Vienna because she could expect to meet with more tolerance, understanding, and openness for her particular problems there.

She was drawn to the great social movements raised by the workers and the youth, and especially to the international women's movement,[11] for which an entirely new era had dawned after the First World War. The effects were especially palpable in "Red Vienna", where the Social Democrats held the absolute majority of votes. The foundation of the republic had granted women the status of citizens, a first in Austrian history. Women were given active and passive suffrage,[12] and the right to assemble in political organisations. These rights did not just exist on paper, but were exercised vigorously. The young republic's first national election for the constitutive National Assembly saw more than eighty-two per cent of all women eligible to vote make use of their newly won right. During the first legislative period, from 1920 to 1923, twelve delegates to the National Council were female—a number that would not be reached again until 1978 (Hauch, 1995, p. 92ff).

The social and political equality of women served as a basic claim of the new democracy. However, there was more at stake: the recognition of a woman as a person in her own right, and the appreciation of her right to autonomy. The Victorian image of women, forged over centuries and until only a few years earlier the model for middle and upper class women without exception, now belonged to Zweig's *World of Yesterday*:

> In the pre-Freudian era therefore, the axiom was agreed upon that a female person could have no physical desires as long as they had not been awakened by man and that, obviously, was officially permitted only in marriage. But even in those moral times, in Vienna in particular, the air was full of dangerous erotic infection, and a girl of good family had to live in a completely sterile atmosphere, from the day of her birth until the day when she left the altar on her husband's arm. In order to protect young girls, they were not left alone for one moment. (Zweig, 1944, p. 79)

Sigmund Freud was not the only contributor to a correction of this image, as Anna Guggenbühl highlights in her first diary entry, an especially striking passage: "I want to go to Russia, like those sons and daughters of the aristocracy left their families at the last revolution, I want to take off and leave this milieu in which I do not belong. I think of this play by Schnitzler, *The Sounding of the Flute* [1911]. Sigmund Freud: This, exactly, is your very conflict."

The allure of the Russian Revolution—the yearning for dissolution of class barriers and generational conflicts—remained unbroken in the year 1921, especially for young people. The latest developments, like the Kronstadt rebellion of February 1921, during which the mutinying sailors arrested the officials of the Soviet administration and seized power over the city, could be read about,[13] but were still difficult to make sense of. In addition, it does not come as a surprise that in her analysis with Freud, Anna Guggenbühl only ever mentions one of Freud's contemporaries by name, at least according to her diary: Arthur Schnitzler, an author she read with great passion.[14] His "Doppelgänger" and "profound psychological researcher", as Freud would address the poet, author, and physician Schnitzler, a year later on his birthday on 14 May 1922, "anticipate[d] [everything] by refined introspection, what he [Freud] uncovered only by laborious investigation into other persons" (Jones, 1962, p. 514). "Your determinism," Freud writes to Schnitzler, "as well as your scepticism—what people call pessimism—your preoccupation with the truth of the unconscious and of the instinctual drives in man, your dissection of the cultural conventions of our society, the dwelling of your thoughts on the polarity of love and death, all this moves me with an uncanny feeling of familiarity" (E. Freud, 1961, p. 345).

The two men shared a critique of bourgeois sexual morals as well as a profound critique of the institution of matrimony, which Freud had already expressed in 1908: "Marital unfaithfulness would ... be a much more probable cure for the neurosis resulting from marriage" (Freud, 1908d, p. 23). In vocally expressing such positions, it is likely that both men really struck a chord with Anna Guggenbühl. Arthur Schnitzler was one of the most successful playwrights of the German-speaking world, who at the time had just caused a sensation with *La Ronde*. Everybody was speaking of the scandal, the newspapers featured extended coverage, and the affair was even treated as the cause of a political crisis. Perhaps it was these stirrings that influenced Guggenbühl when writing her diary, as the work she refers to is neither *The Sounding of the Flute* nor is it a play. It is rather a novella titled *The Shepherd's Pipe* (Schnitzler, 1911).[15]

What Anna Guggenbühl remembered was thus not the "typical novelistic object-symbol" (Fliedl, 2005, p. 162) but the sweet sound of seduction: "maybe this sound of the flute is the one single lure that you are ready to succumb to, or maybe it is only one of a few or of many" (Schnitzler, 1911, p. 236).[16] In the novella, the aged Erasmus, in a spirit of overly rational liberalism, sets his young wife Dionysia free, and suggests she should give in to seduction: "This is the sounding of the shepherd's flute. And behold, without willing to confess to it, yes even without fully realising, you, who in this instant were still ready to go to your death, are moved to a longing to know which pair of lips is caressing the flute whose call is resounding" (ibid.). Dionysia lives through Anna Guggenbühl's "Leporello's aria"—as Freud calls his analysand's fantasies about the men she would like to have relations with—in a "revue of female figures of different social and moral standing, ranging from wife to shepherd's playmate, industrialist's companion, worker's harlot, and lover of a count to mistress of a prince" (Fliedl, 2005, p. 163), none of which would allow her to find her happiness. It is also for this reason that Dionysia finally leaves her husband, as she is disgusted "by the stony mask of his wisdom" (Schnitzler, 1911, p. 261), that is, by his mock understanding for her erotic needs, which only objectifies her once more without taking her seriously as an autonomous person (cf., Fliedl, 2005, p. 164). The young Swiss woman felt encouraged by Schnitzler's writing and Freud's thinking to undertake a similar step.

While Dionysia's journey of experience is still set in a "fairy-tale realm of dreams"[17] (Fliedl), Schnitzler's *La Ronde* (original German name, *Reigen*), a tragicomedy in ten acts, introduced an open, mirror-like criticism of the hypocritical "civilised sexual morality" with a biting realism. The play shook the already slowly decaying foundations of this morality, and caused one of the greatest scandals in the history of theatre. Arthur Schnitzler had finished *La Ronde* in 1897 but deemed the play unfit for public performance; he self-published a first edition of 200 copies in 1900 at his own expense. The subsequent publication as a book in 1903 garnered great attention, and culminated in the release of ten additional editions in eight months, which amounted to 14,000 copies sold. Still, the author allowed its theatrical performance only after the war. The premiere took place on 23 December 1920, at the Kleines Schauspielhaus in Berlin. In Vienna, the play opened on 1 February 1921 at the Kammerspiele.

Ten dialogues between a man and a woman, each divided into a "before" and an "after", the climax of each centrally marked by what amounts to perhaps the most fatal dashes in the history of literature. Given as "— — — — — " in the manuscript[18] (Schnitzler, 1903, p. 10ff), they were rendered as lights out or a fall of the curtain on stage, and thus let the sexual act manifest as a silent, yet lively image in the audience's fantasy. With the sexual encounters of different social classes—between harlot-soldier, soldier-parlour maid, parlour maid-young gentleman, young gentleman-young wife, young wife-husband, husband-*Süßes Mädel*,[19] *Süßes Mädel*-poet, poet-actress, actress-count, count-harlot— Schnitzler stages the circle of *La Ronde* as closed. In the middle, though not at the centre of the play, stands the bourgeois conjugal bed, which gives insight into the factitiousness of the dominant sexual morality: "The Husband: I've only loved one woman: you. A man can only love where he finds purity and truth" (Schnitzler, 1903, p. 52).[20]

The Berlin premiere already foreshadowed what should finally escalate in Vienna. The performance was met with vocal protest against "the licentious concoction of the Jew from Vienna",[21] which even led to litigation (see Pfoser, Pfoser-Schewig, & Renner, 1993). The lifting of a temporary injunction in Berlin on 6 January 1921 could not quell the protests. They were only the harbingers of the Viennese scandal, and as such also the precursors to the future political catastrophe. In Berlin, it was the *Verband nationalgesinnter Soldaten* (Union of Nationally-Minded Soldiers) and the *Antisemitischer Schutz- und Trutzbund*, (Antisemitic League for Protection and Defence), who sabotaged *La Ronde*. During the arrests, the protesters were singing "Deutschland über alles", and chanted slogans like "Down with the Jews!"[22]

In Vienna, the national-conservative and the *völkisch* (populist) press had stirred up anti-Semitic sentiments against the author and the play by using terms like "pornographer" or "Jewish swine-litterateur". The Christian Social Party member of parliament, and later federal chancellor, prelate Ignaz Seipel, classified the atmosphere according to party politics, when he remarked at an assembly of Catholics "that the Social Democrats have to appear and stage tempestuous scenes, as long as it serves the defence of some Jewish machinations."[23] Right afterwards, Schnitzler relates in his diary that over 300 demonstrators marched to the Kammerspiele, "insulted the theatregoers, who were just arriving, and yelled: 'They violate our women! Down with *La Ronde*! Down with the Social Democrats'" (Schnitzler, 2006, p. 43).[24] After further demonstrations and attempted disruptions of the play, the performance of 16 February 1921 had to be interrupted and cancelled, an event that— at least from the viewpoint of the *Neue Freie Presse*—"could have been forecast with mathematical certitude."[25] The incidents were unique: noticeable agitation emerged "already during the first dialogues, as a sharp, pungent stench, which could be discerned as caused by stink bombs, gradually announced itself". During the performance, demonstrators entered the building, which resulted in:

> physical assaults on many patrons, on men and women, who were beaten and pulled by their hair … suddenly a jet of water poured over the auditorium, after a demonstrator had opened the fire hydrant that was closest to the stage … the guards were attacked with sticks and clubs … men who wanted to protect their women against the intimidation were beaten up, many of them were injured by blows from batons and brass knuckles, female patrons were pulled to the ground and dragged over it by their hair.[26]

While demonstrations, protests, and scenes of turmoil later also took place in Munich, Hamburg, Frankfurt, Hannover, Eisenach, Mährisch-Ostrau, Prague, and so on, they were nowhere as violent and serious as in Vienna. After all subsequent performances of *La Ronde* were officially banned by the police, the conflict about the play grew into a cultural struggle between "Red Vienna" and the federal government, which was dominated by the Christian Social Party. The debate soon turned into a matter of grave national importance, and indicated a crisis in the young constitution. Passionate scenes became the order of the day in the Austrian National Assembly and the Landtag of Vienna. The conflicts of competence surrounding the ban of the public performance of *La Ronde*, which unfolded between the "black" ministry of internal affairs and the "red" municipality of Vienna, were an early and most visible demonstration of the dynamics of tension that would exacerbate dramatically from July 1927 onwards, and finally split the country in the civil war of February 1934.[27]

The first six months of 1921, during which Anna Guggenbühl lived in Vienna, was a culturally, socially, and politically exciting period. In the European metropolis of two million inhabitants, Guggenbühl not only witnessed the fall of the monarchy and its old order that had lasted for centuries, but also the struggle of the nascent workers', youth and women's movement, which pointed to the future. She was confronted with poverty, hunger (Coriat, 1921), and a severe shortage of housing, but also encountered the first social experiments of the Austro-Marxist municipality. She experienced an open, everyday anti-Semitism and the clash of two politically organised ideologies, which continuously threatened to make the latent tendencies towards a civil war very real.

The focus of her personal experience most probably lay in witnessing the effect of two men who, each in their own way, brought forward the correlation of a hypocritical "civilised sexual morality and modern nervous illness", and whose critique opened up an expanded range of opportunities in terms of taking charge of one's own life—especially for women.

Notes

1. Korrespondenzblatt der Internationalen Psychoanalytischen Vereinigung. Sitzungsbericht. In: *Internationale Zeitschrift für Psychoanalyse (1920)*: 382.

2. Rank, O. (1921). *Letter to the Committee, March 1*. Otto Rank Collection, Columbia University, New York, New York. The hard currency that Anna Guggenbühl would have paid for her treatment was certainly one of the reasons why Freud accepted her for analysis. To me, another significant factor appears to be the fact that in his close contact with the young doctor, Freud hoped to access thoughts and experiences similar to those of his beloved daughter Sophie, who was born in the same year as Anna Guggenbühl, and had died at the age of 26 on 26 January 1920.

3. See *Arbeiter-Zeitung* of 25 April 1921 ("The Tyrolean referendum for annexation. Tremendous participation—nearly 99% for Germany") and of 30 May 1921 ("The Salzburg referendum. Nearly unanimous 'Yes'").

4. Translator's note: the German saying "jemandem die Rede verschlagen" literally, to "beat the speech away from someone", has an implicitly violent feel that is lost in the English phrase, which only "leaves" someone speechless.

5. A general interest for the group as a psychological phenomenon also became apparent in the wide distribution of Freud's work. Only three years after its initial publication, a second edition of 6,000–10,000 was printed. In 1922, the English translation was introduced to the market.

In 1923, a Russian translation was announced as being "prepared for the press". Apparently, this edition could no longer be published, as the Stalin regime had gradually yet firmly receded from psychoanalysis, a school of thought that Leo Trotsky had cherished. In 1924, came French, Spanish, and Dutch translations, followed in 1929 by a Japanese translation.

6. As Mario Erdheim has pointed out (1982), Freud's "group psychology" is predominantly a "psychology of institutions", and should also be read as a radical critique of institutional formations. While the more modern, and more recently relevant example of the political parties is not yet directly addressed in Freud's critical discussion of the church and the army, they should nevertheless be kept in mind continuously.

7. Translator's note: to preserve the peculiarities of this special source, I have adopted the jumbled grammar of the original German protocol.

8. Translator's note: anagogic means another way of dream interpretation compared to the psychoanalytic method.

9. Freud–Eitingon letters, Freud Museum London. Translated by KPH.

10. Sigmund Freud Papers, Sigmund Freud Collection, Manuscript Division. Library of Congress. Washington DC. Translated by KPH.

11. Throughout her life, Anna Guggenbühl identified with the movement for the emancipation of women and, in the late 1920s, authored a number of feminist papers (personal correspondence with Anna Koellreuter).

12. In Switzerland, national suffrage for women was only established in 1971.

13. "The mutiny of the Kronstadt sailors". *Neue Freie Presse*, 14 February 1921, p. 1.

14. Personal correspondence with Anna Koellreuter.

15. I thank Konstanze Fliedl for her significant advice.

16. Translator's note: translation of all quotations in this paragraph by KPH.

17. Translator's note: translation of Fliedl by KPH.

18. The dashes were also subject of contemporary censorship reports: "Namely those scenes that are marked with dashes in the manuscript, have to be contained in such manner, that the spectator is spared the perception of the sensual instance." The censorship reports for *La Ronde. Arbeiter-Zeitung*, 24 April 1921.

19. Translator's note: this literary type (literally "sweet missy") marks a sexually approachable young woman of the lower classes, often residing in the Vienna suburbs.

20. Translator's note: quotation translated by Eric Bentley, see *La Ronde* paperback edition, New York: Samuel French, 2011.

21. Translator's note: translation of Pfoser et al. by KPH.
22. "The *La Ronde* scandals in Berlin." *Neue Freie Presse*, 23 February 1921, p. 5.
23. "Delegate Professor Dr. Seipl about the 'La Ronde' affair." In: *Neue Freie Presse*, 14 February 1921.
24. Translator's note: quotation translated by KPH.
25. "Disruption of today's performance of *La Ronde*. Stink bombs and violent scuffles in the auditorium—night show called off". *Neue Freie Presse*, 17 February 1921.
26. All quotations in *Neue Freie Presse*, 17 February 1921, p. 7.
27. After all the scandal, Schnitzler himself banned public performances of his play; the ban was only lifted by his son Heinrich Schnitzler on 1 January 1982.

References

Bernfeld, S. (1914). *Die neue Jugend und die Frauen*. Vienna: Kamoenenverlag.
Coriat, I. H. (1921). Sex and hunger. *Psychoanalytic Review, 8*: 375–381.
Erdheim, M. (1982). *Die gesellschaftliche Produktion von Unbewusstheit. Eine Einführung in den ethnopsychoanalytischen Prozess*. Frankfurt: Suhrkamp.
Fallend, K. (1992). Von der Jugendbewegung zur Psychoanalyse. In: K. Fallend & J. Reichmayr (Eds.), *Siegfried Bernfeld oder die Grenzen der Psychoanalyse* (pp. 48–69). Frankfurt: Stroemfeld.
Fallend, K. (1995). *Sonderlinge, Träumer, Sensitive: Psychoanalyse auf dem Weg zur Institution und Profession. Protokolle der Wiener Psychoanalytischen Vereinigung und biographische Studien*. Vienna: Jugend & Volk.
Federn, P. (1919). Zur Psychologie der Revolution: Die vaterlose Gesellschaft. In: H. Dahmer (Ed.), *Analytische Sozialpsychologie (Volume 1)* (pp. 65–87). Frankfurt: Suhrkamp.
Fliedl, K. (2005). *Arthur Schnitzler*. Stuttgart: Reclam.
Freud, A. (1968). Schwierigkeiten der Psychoanalyse in Vergangenheit und Gegenwart. In: *Die Schriften der Anna Freud, Bd. IX* (pp. 2,481–2,508). Frankfurt: Fischer, 1987.
Freud, E. (Ed.) (1961). *Letters of Sigmund Freud, 1873–1939*. T. Stern & J. Stern (Trans.). New York: Basic.
Freud, S. (1908d). "Civilized" Sexual Morality and Modern Nervous Illness. *S. E., 9*: 179. London: Hogarth.
Freud, S. (1921c). *Group Psychology and the Analysis of the Ego. S. E., 18*: (pp. 69–143). London: Hogarth.
Groddeck, G. (1921). *Der Seelensucher: Ein psychoanalytischer Roman*. Wiesbaden: Limes, 1971.

Hauch, G. (1995). *Vom Frauenstandpunkt aus: Frauen im Parlament 1919–1933.* Vienna: Verlag für Gesellschaftskritik.

Hauch, G. (2008). Welche Welt? Welche Politik? Zum Geschlecht in Revolte, Rätebewegung, Parteien und Parlament. In: H. Konrad. & W. Maderthaner (Eds.), *Das Werden der Republik* (pp. 317–338). Vienna: Carl Gerold's Sohn.

Jones, E. (1962). *Das Leben und Werk von Sigmund Freud. Band III. Die letzte Phase 1919–1939.* Bern: Hans Huber, 1978.

Pfoser, A., Pfoser-Schewig, K., & Renner, G. (Eds.) (1993). *Schnitzlers "Reigen". Analysen und Dokumente. Band 1: der Skandal. Band 2: Die Prozesse.* Frankfurt: Fischer.

Schnitzler, A. (1903). *Reigen: Zehn Dialoge.* Stuttgart: Reclam, 2007.

Schnitzler, A. (1911). *Die Hirtenflöte.* Stuttgart: Deutscher Bücherbund, 1975.

Schnitzler, A. (2006). *Reigen: Zehn Dialoge.* In: Burgtheater Wien, theatre programme.

Teslin, E. (1919). *Massenpsychologie und Selbsterkenntnis.* Olten: Verlag.

Zweig, S. (1944). *The World of Yesterday. (Reprint edition).* A. Bell (Trans.). Lincoln, NE: University of Nebraska Press, 2013.

CHAPTER FIVE

Freud the analyst and therapist

Ernst Falzeder

"If our aim continues to be to verbalise the nascent conscious in terms of the transference, then we are practising analysis; if not, then we are analysts practising something else that we deem to be appropriate to the occasion. And why not?"

—*Winnicott*, 1962, p. 170

"In analysis, one can do anything; one only has to be sure about what is done, why, and to which ends."

—*Caruso, in Tanco-Duque*, 1988, p. 78

Freud never published a comprehensive work about psycho-analytical technique. Though he did entertain plans of writing a "general methodology", he finally gave them up.[1] The smaller articles that emerged instead (Freud, 1911 1915) did not give hard "rules" but were rather formulated as "advice". They were also, as he would later notice himself, "entirely inadequate", helpful only for "beginners" (Blanton, 1971, p. 48), and "essentially negative" (Freud & Ferenczi, 2000, p. 332): they outlined what analysts should *not* do, rather than formulating positive principles.

For a long time, little was known about Freud's own analytic methods, which opened the floodgates for fantasies of all kinds. For instance, it was often tacitly assumed that he practised according to the recommendations that he published, which sometimes, underhandedly, elevated these "recommendations" into general, authoritative "dos and don'ts". This image, however, is increasingly challenged by the publication of unabbreviated correspondence, of memoirs, of interviews, and of other documents. New material of this sort keeps surfacing, and forces us to continuously reconsider the question of Freud's method.

At present, a diverse range of sources allows insights into Freud's way of working:

Texts by Freud himself

In addition to his clinical histories and case notes (e.g., Freud, 1955a), Freud left a wealth of letters, in which he not only reflects upon his practice but also provides supervision for his followers.

Memoirs by former analysands

Relatively many of Freud's former analysands have recorded and published recollections of their analysis, among them Smiley Blanton (1971), Helene Deutsch (1973), John Dorsey (1976), Roy Grinker (1975, 1979), "H. D." [Hilda Doolittle] (1956), Abram Kardiner (1977), Kata Lévy-Freund (1990), Sergej Pankejeff (in Gardiner, 1971; cf. Obholzer, 1980), Adolph Stern (1922), Bruno Walter (1946), and Joseph Wortis (1984) (also cf. Ruitenbeek, 1973). Further recollections still remain unpublished, for instance those of the painter and graphic artist Rudolf Kriser (1954), and the exhaustive diaries Marie Bonaparte kept about her analysis (see Bertin, 1982). The most detailed among the records that have been published to date are probably those of Ernst Blum, which the analysand put down after each session with Freud's consent (Pohlen, 2006).

Interviews with former analysands

Here, the work of Kurt Eissler and Paul Roazen is most notable, as both have conducted many interviews with former analysands of Freud's, albeit with different intentions in mind. By his own account, Roazen interrogated twenty-five former patients (1995, p. xviii) and processed the information thus gathered in several books and articles (cf., Roazen, 1971, 1992, 1995). The transcripts of Eissler's interviews (Library of Congress, Sigmund Freud Collection) are still only partly accessible even today, although some of them have been assessed in first exploratory publications. Drawing on an unpublished autobiography and on one of Eissler's interviews, for instance, David Lynn has written about Freud's analysis of Emma Eckstein's nephew Albert Hirst (Lynn, 1997). In cooperation with George Vaillant, Lynn has also analysed forty-three of Freud's cases in terms of how Freud dealt with anonymity, neutrality, and confidentiality (Lynn & Vaillant, 1998).

Reports in secondary literature

From secondary literature, we know, for instance, of Freud's therapeutic intervention with Gustav Mahler (Jones, 1955, pp. 79–80). As becomes apparent in this case and others—for instance with Bruno Walter[2] and Bruno Götz[3] (see Gay, 1988, pp. 166–167; Goldmann, 1985)—Freud without doubt engaged in therapeutic as well as analytical work.[4]

Freud's patient calendars

Some years ago, Christfried Tögel drew attention to a relevant source that had previously gone unnoticed: namely, Freud's calendars kept at the Freud Museum in London, which document patient appointments for the time between October 1910 and December 1920 without any gaps. Tögel himself (2009) and Ulrike May (2006, 2007a, 2007b, 2008) have made first attempts at analysing this fascinating material, which seems recalcitrant only at the first glance. With these three calendars, "we have at our disposal a protocol of about ten years of his therapeutic activity, which provides us with previously inconceivable opportunities to inform ourselves about his practice extensively and meticulously" (May, 2006, p. 43).

Sigmund Freud not only introduced a completely new perspective for addressing mental life, but also developed the very instrument that made such research possible. This instrument is called psychoanalysis.[5] What, now, is psychoanalysis in this sense? Freud's answer: "The session ... proceeds like a conversation between two people equally awake, but one of whom is spared every muscular exertion and every distracting sensory impression which might divert his attention from his own mental activity" (Freud, 1904a, p. 250). In 1926, he corroborates: "Nothing takes place between them except they talk to each other" (Freud, 1926e, p. 187).

The partner in this conversation, the analysand, is encouraged to "'let himself go' in what he says, 'as you would do in a conversation in which you were rambling on quite disconnectedly and at random'" (Freud, 1904a, p. 251), and to "act as though, for instance, you were a traveller sitting next to the window of a railway carriage and describing to someone inside the carriage the changing views which you see outside" (Freud, 1913c, p. 135). On the other hand, the analyst should "not direct ... one's notice to anything in particular and ... maintain ... the same 'evenly suspended attention'" (Freud, 1912e, p. 111). Nothing is too insubstantial or embarrassing to keep it from being noticed and addressed. On the contrary! It is this radical honesty that sets Freud's method apart: "analysis ... is in the first place an honest establishment of the facts" (Freud & Pfister, 1963, p. 87).

Both requirements—to talk and to listen minutely and attentively— provoke resistance. This honesty sets out to *perceive* with as little prejudice as possible, an endeavour that the individual nevertheless tries to counter "by every possible critical expedient, until at last he feels positive discomfort" (Freud, 1904a, p. 251). Potent affective powers protect the core of the impulses and imaginations that are staved off, around which the free associations keep pulsing, forever beating around the bush. Freud has thus "developed ... an *art of interpretation*" (Freud, 1904a, p. 252) that should allow access to the original meaning of what is said.

When Freud published his programmatic article *Freud's Psycho-Analytic Procedure* (1904a), he had already experienced in practice how these affective powers could also be channelled into "transference". Three years earlier, he had addressed this in the Dora analysis:

> What are transferences? They are new editions or facsimiles of the impulses and phantasies which are aroused and made conscious during the progress of the analysis; but they have this peculiarity, which is characteristic for their species, that they replace some earlier person by the person of the physician. To put it another way: A whole series of psychological experiences are revived ... as applying to the person of the physician at the present moment. (Freud, 1905e, p. 116)

While he had initially probably provoked it without intention,[6] Freud later recognises transference as a fundamental component of the analytic encounter. After all, in the same essay, he postulates that once one is aware of transference, it is the "most powerful ally" to analysis (ibid., p. 117).

In his own words, Freud set out "to understand something of the riddles of the world in which we live and perhaps even contribute to their solution" (Freud, 1927a, p. 253)—human riddles, as we may assume, even though he claims to have "no knowledge of ... any craving ... to help suffering humanity" (ibid., p. 253). As he was taught in his training, it was his scientific ideal to create a laboratory-like situation, which would allow him to observe the phenomena unfolding there without asserting any influence on them himself. In his study of "human conditions", this scientific ideal necessarily clashed with his own needs and his personal ideas of morality; a morality that he always regarded as something "that goes without saying" (Freud, 1905a, p. 267). Freud was forced to develop a number of defences that would help him deal with the affects emerging in the therapeutic relationship. In a letter to Ferenczi's lover Gizella Pálos, for instance, he described himself as "hard-hearted" (Freud & Ferenczi, 1993, p. 321)—however, as he was quick to add, "out of sympathy and softness" (ibid.). He saw himself as "a sensitive ass [who] never ceases making a fool of himself, even when he has grey hair" (ibid., p. 333).

From many sources, we know that Freud allowed in his treatments for a sphere in which he did not act "abstinent", but in which he could react in a spontaneous, moralistic, hurt, angry, loving, lecturing, or effervescent manner. About his former patient E., for instance, he wrote to Fliess: "He demonstrated the reality of my theory in my own case, providing me in a surprising reversal with the solution, which I had overlooked, to my former railroad phobia. For this piece of work I even made him the present of a picture of Oedipus and the Sphinx" (Freud, 1985, pp. 391–392). Another example: Albert Hirst's analysis began in 1903, when Hirst was sixteen years old. Freud encouraged Hirst to sit down on the chair in the exact position that he took when he masturbated. He assured Hirst that masturbation was not a harmful activity, which greatly relieved the patient (Lynn, 1997, p. 74).

In Freud's notes on the case of the "Rat Man" we can read that he repeatedly thought it "necessary" to "give [his patient] a piece of the theory" (Freud, 1955a, p. 522), that he made him "compliment[s] for the lucidity with which he expresses those states" (ibid., p. 521),[7] and that he demanded his patient bring a photograph of his lady, which led to complications ("Violent struggle, bad day. Resistance"; ibid., p. 260). We also learn what his analysand thought about a postcard sent to him by Freud, namely, that "signed 'cordially' was too intimate" (ibid., p. 293), and that Freud "gave him Zola's *Joie de Vivre* to read" (ibid., p. 306). Freud also writes: "Once when he had told me that his girl had lain on her stomach and her genital hairs were visible from behind, I had said to him that it was a pity that women nowadays gave no care to them and spoke of them as unlovely" (ibid., p. 311). Freud even treated his patient to dinner[8] ("He was hungry and was fed", ibid., p. 303)—the host served herring. In the following session, "there was a transference phantasy. Between two women—my wife and my mother—a herring was stretched, extending from the anus of one to that of the other. A girl cut it in two ... All he could say at first was that he disliked herrings intensely ... The girl was one he had seen on the stairs and had taken to be my twelve-year-old daughter" (ibid., pp. 307–308). The patient then confessed to Freud that he had been suspicious from very early on in the therapy, since "[h]e knew, he said, that a great misfortune had once befallen my family: a brother of mine, who was a waiter, had committed a murder in Budapest and been executed for it. I asked him with a laugh how he knew that, whereupon his whole affect collapsed" (ibid., p. 285).

There are also a number of reports that account for Freud's activities in later years. Abram Kardiner, for instance, writes: "At the end of the fifth month, March [1922], he began saying: '*Herr Doktor, ein bischen* (sic) *Durcharbeitung* [working through].' Now, this idea caused me a good deal of bewilderment ... From this point on, the analysis drifted" (Kardiner, 1977, pp. 62–63). About Clarence Oberndorf's analysis with Freud, Kardiner relates how Freud stubbornly insisted on one of his interpretations: "This interpretation infuriated Oberndorf, and they haggled about this dream for months, until Freud got tired of it and discontinued the analysis" (ibid., p. 76). "The fact that Freud talked to me excited a good deal of attention in Vienna, so much that one day I was honored with an invitation to tea by James Strachey and John Rickman ... John Rickman said to me, 'I understand Freud talks to you.' I said, 'Yes, he does, all the time.' They said: 'Well, how do you do it?' I answered, 'I don't exactly know ... How is it with you?' They both said, 'He never says a word'" (ibid., pp. 77–78).

Obviously, to Freud, analysis was not a realm beyond morality, as he remarked to Smiley Blanton: "Es gibt in der Analyse nichts, was menschlichen Errungenschaften und moralischer Würde Abbruch tut" (Blanton, 1971). On 13 February 1930, Freud makes Blanton a present of a volume of his collected works—not without adding that Blanton "aus der Lektüre Gewinn ziehen würde" (Blanton, 1971). John Dorsey, who was in analysis with Freud between 1935 and 1937, related, for instance: "I recall during a session his leaning over the couch and singing [!] one or two strains to me from Mozart's *Don Giovanni*" (Dorsey, 1976, p. 51). And what happened in this one session (1933) that Hilda Doolittle recalls?

> I did not know what enraged him suddenly. I veered round off the couch, my feet on the floor … The professor himself is uncanonical enough; he is beating with his hand, with his fist on the head-piece of the old-fashioned horsehair sofa … And even as I veered around, facing him, my mind was detached enough to wonder if this was some idea of *his* for speeding up the analytic content or redirecting the flow of associated images. The Professor said, "The trouble is—I am an old man—*you do not think it worth your while to love me.*" (Doolittle, 1956, pp. 15–16, italics in original)

And, in a letter to Doolittle: "What you gave me was not praise, was [sic] affection and I need not be ashamed of my satisfaction. Life at my age is not easy, but spring is beautiful and so is love" (ibid., p. 197).

Let us remember in this context that Freud did not want to take on a maternal role.

> He had said, "And, I must tell you (you were frank with me and I will be frank with you), I do *not* like to be the mother in transference—it always surprises and shocks me a little. I feel so very masculine." I asked him if others had what he called this mother-transference on him. He said ironically and I thought a little wistfully, "Oh, *very* many." (Doolittle, 1956, p. 52, italics in original)

Similarly, he told Kardiner, "that I am too much the father" (Kardiner, 1977, p. 69). To Groddeck: "Your putting of my person in the mother sequence—into which I obviously do not fit—… shows clearly how you want to evade the father transference" (Freud & Groddeck, 1974, p. 59).[9]

Let us also recall that Freud did not like psychotics: "I finally admitted to myself that I did not like those patients ... They make me angry and I find myself irritated to experience them so distant from myself and from all that is human. This is an astonishing intolerance which brands me a poor psychiatrist ... Do I act like earlier doctors acted against the hysterics, could my attitude result from my ever increasing partisanship for the primate of the intellect, from a hostility towards the Id? Or what else might it be?" (Letter to István Hollós, in Schur, 1966, p. 10; Dupont, 1988, p. 251)[10]

In multiple instances, he made disparaging remarks about his "nuts" (Freud & Jung, 1974, p. 359) and "fools" (Freud & Ferenczi, 1996, p. 252), and "shared with only a trusted few" his "pessimistic view" that the "neurotics are rabble, good only to support us financially and to allow us to learn from their cases; psychoanalysis as a therapy may be worthless" (Ferenczi, 1932, pp. 185–186). To Binswanger's question about his position towards his patients, Freud answered: "I could wring their necks, all of them" (Binswanger, 1956, p. 56). To Fließ, he wrote: "When I am not cheerful and collected, every single one of my patients is my tormentor. I really believed I would have to give up on the sot" (Freud, 1985, p. 404). To Edoardo Weiss: "Consider furthermore that, regretfully, only a few patients are worth the trouble we spend on them, so that we are not allowed to have a therapeutic attitude, but we must be glad to have learned something in every case" (Weiss, 1991, p. 37).

If, however, he felt that someone was close to him and "the cause", Freud could act almost affectionately. The members of the secret committee he called his "children" or his "adopted children" (Freud & Ferenczi, 1993, pp. 463 and 465). He advised Ferenczi, with whom Jones was in analysis at the time: "Be strict and tender with him [Jones]. He is a very good person. Feed the pupa so that a queen can be made out of it" (ibid., p. 490). About Ernst Jones's girlfriend Loe Kann, who had her analysis with Freud at the same time, he confessed: "This Loe has become extraordinarily dear to me, and I have produced with her a very warm feeling with complete sexual inhibition, as has rarely been the case before (probably owing to my age)" (ibid., p. 499). During Kann's analysis, Jones was sleeping with her nurse and companion Lina, which led Freud to remark that he still respected Jones highly, who, after all, was able to work through the episode in analysis, and thus provided the analyst with an interesting—if dangerous—experiment (ibid., 466).

It is well known that when the so-called Wolf Man lost his fortune, Freud supported him financially. "Freud also encouraged Bruno Goetz, who suffered from facial neuralgia in 1904, to self-education, and gave him 200 *Kronen* on top of his recipe for painkillers, so that he could afford to buy a beef steak every once in a while" (Goldmann, 1985, p. 316). Dr Max Graf, father of "Little Hans", tells the following tale: His second wife was in analysis with Freud, and got in trouble with her parents. Her mother announced "she would no longer pay for treatment. Then the young lady went to Freud and said: 'Professor Freud, unfortunately I cannot continue with the treatment, can I; you see, I don't have the funds for it.' And Freud told her: 'Why, and you cannot bring yourself to continue with the treatment as a poor girl?' And she accepted this, you know?! He treated her without taking any payment for it" (Interview with Kurt Eissler on 16 December 1952, Library of Congress, Manuscript Division).

On the other hand, Freud did not hold back from judging others during an analysis. "About Dr. Horney, he said: She is able but malicious—mean" (Blanton, 1971, p. 65). His involvement went so far that he interfered substantially with his students' and analysands' private lives: Pfister, for instance, he strongly encouraged to divorce from his wife (Freud & Jung, 1974); Horace Frink he pressured into leaving his wife to marry someone else (see Edmunds, 1988); Ferenczi he tried to keep from marrying Elma Pálos; Helene Deutsch he advised to end the analysis of Viktor Tausk, a request with which she obliged (see Roazen, 1969)—interferences that in many cases brought with them uncomfortable, at times even devastating, effects.

From these records emerges a multi-faceted—if probably still somewhat distorted and incomplete—image of Freud the therapist.[11] Without analysing, judging or weighing these reports too much, it can still be observed that Freud was obviously very reserved in some cases, whereas he got extraordinarily involved in others. They show that he did get involved with patients that interested him, that he gave them gifts or offered them jobs (for instance, translations); and that he did not hide his personality doing so, but often enough made use of it in the process. This contrasts strongly with his published statements, in which he generally recommended a much more conservative stance.

In other words, in practice Freud broke his own prohibitions so often that it would be grossly misleading to read his methodological publications as reliable sources that described how he actually worked. It almost seems as if with him, these aberrations were not the exception, but the rule.[12] Considering the blunders that his sorcerer's apprentices stumbled into at times, he could act the part of their "venerable old master" (Freud & Jung, 1974, p. 290), who was free to ignore his own advice should it not fit an occasion for whatever reason.

On the other hand, he also conceded that his students need not stick fast to all these rules—a fact that is perhaps not acknowledged widely enough. To give only one example: when his analysand Irmarita Putnam told him about a female patient of hers for whom she had done all kinds of things that violated the "rule" of abstinence (she had, for instance, given her money, and had an artist paint her portrait), Freud said: "Sometimes one has to be both mother and father to a patient." And: "You do what you can." According to Putnam, Freud was "completely unorthodox". To Freud, the only thing that mattered was that the analyst's measure "did not mean some personal gratification for the analyst but was in the interest of the patient" (Roazen, 1995, pp. 192–193). It is more important what one is for a patient, than what one does for him (Bertin, 1982, p. 291).[13]

Freud was not only flexible regarding his "technique", but also in the choice of the setting. This does not only apply to Max Eitingon's famous "analysis" in walking (similarly, the therapeutic intervention with Gustav Mahler had taken place while on a four-hour stroll), but it was indeed characteristic. Freud's practice generally distinguished itself in that he did not offer the same "standard" analysis to everyone (x hours per week for a minimum duration of x months) but tended to customise sessions according to the needs of individual cases and of himself, as well as requirements dictated by particular circumstances— for instance, when an analysand would come in from abroad, or when they only had limited time or money at their disposal. Duration and frequency of treatment varied greatly: between 1910 and 1920 alone, we find analyses that lasted between a couple of days and many years, that needed only a few sittings or over 1,000 hours, and that required between three and nineteen-and-a-half (!) hours per week (May, 2007a, 2007b).

Among all these sources, the diary of the analysis that is published here for the first time in English takes a very particular place: first, it documents a therapeutic intervention and not a so-called training analysis;[14] second, it took place before Freud was diagnosed with cancer;

and third, it consists of notes that seem to document word for word snippets of what was said in the consulting room. While there are many other documents that fulfil one or the other of these criteria, none of the previously published accounts meets all three of them. The by far largest part culls from the accounts of analysands undergoing analysis as a necessary part of their training to become analysts themselves. Most of those analyses took place after Freud was operated on for cancer, which notably affected his "technique": he became hard of hearing in one of his ears, and speaking was difficult and even painful for him. As a consequence, he appeared more reticent, which is perhaps also due to the fact that most of these analyses were conducted in English.[15] And finally, only a few of these records contain such a detailed protocol of the therapeutic dialogue as Anna Guggenbühl's diary does.

This book illustrates how Freud worked in this particular case. In general, it can be said that Anna's report does not fundamentally challenge our more recent conception of the clinical Freud that has slowly built up during the last years and decades. It does, however, provide additional facets to this image—and it remains a pleasure to be able to look into Freud's practice over his shoulder (cf. Cremerius, 1981). We can only be grateful to Anna Koellreuter and her mother—Anna Guggenbühl's daughter—for deciding to share this valuable document with the interested public.

Notes

1. A first mention of Freud's plan to draft a "General Methodology of Psychoanalysis" can be found in his letter to Abraham of 9 January 1908 (Freud & Abraham, 2002, p. 20). He pursued the project until 1910, when he abandoned it in its comprehensive form, and, between 1911 and 1915, published a series of short articles instead (cf., the editor's introduction to Freud, 1985, pp. 85–88).
2. One of the most important conductors of the twentieth century.
3. A Swiss poet who attended university in Vienna at the time.
4. "Il n'y a pas de doute que Freud avait une activité psychothérapeutique, même dans les années de maturité" [There is no doubt that Freud acted as a psychotherapist, even in his mature years] (Haynal, 2007, p. 242).
5. "What characterizes psycho-analysis as a science is not the material which it handles but the technique with which it works ... What it aims at and achieves is nothing other than the uncovering of what is unconscious in mental life" (Freud, 1916–1917, p. 389).

6. He initially understood transference as an interfering factor, or even, in the Dora case, as the reason for why treatment can fail.

7. Translator's note: the two quotations from Freud, 1955a, are missing in the English *Standard Edition*. Translation from the German version by KPH.

8. This was not the first such invitation, either: one female patient L. G. "was my guest one evening, and will be invited regularly" (Freud, 1985, p. 406). "E. at last concluded his career as a patient by coming to dinner at my house" (ibid., p. 409).

9. Translator's note: translation from the German by Peter L. Rudnytsky (2002, p. 156).

10. Translator's note: as only part of the paragraph quoted here exists in English translation in Dupont, 1988, the translation above is a composite of Dupont's and my own.

11. There are many books and articles dealing with the development of Freud's technique, which could not be addressed here. The most comprehensive overview so far, which also looks back at procedures of psychoanalytic treatment before 1920 on a more general level, can be found in Leitner (2001).

12. Paul Roazen even suggests that the gap between what Freud recommended in public and what he practised was so great that it necessitated a "conspiracy of silence" among those of his followers who were aware of it (Roazen, 1995, p. xxii).

13. "Plus important que ce que l'on fait est ce que l'on est." This is my translation of the French original text, as the German translation twists the sentence around and changes its meaning: "Wichtiger als das, was man ist, ist das, was man macht" (p. 315). With thanks to André Haynal.

14. Even if the difference between these procedures was not at all clearly cut in the early days of psychoanalysis. In Guggenbühl's case it is evident that she sought treatment to make a decision about the relationship to her fiancé, not to become an analyst herself.

15. "[T]he most significant single event in Freud's life as a practicing analyst was his getting cancer of the jaw in 1923; among those I met who had been in analysis with Freud that even constituted a genuine watershed. Significantly, he never wrote another case history afterward … [He was] altogether less outgoing than before in his clinical practice. It now hurt Freud to talk" (Roazen, 1992, p. 293).

References

Bertin, C. (1982). *Marie Bonaparte*. Paris: Plon, 1999.

Binswanger, L. (1956). *Erinnerungen an Sigmund Freud*. Bern: Francke.

Blanton, S. (1971). *Diary of My Analysis with Freud*. New York: Hawthorn.

Cremerius, J. (1981). Freud bei der Arbeit über die Schulter geschaut: Seine Technik im Spiegel von Schülern und Patienten. *Jahrbuch der Psychoanalyse, Beiheft 6*: 123–158.

Deutsch, H. (1973). *Confrontations with Myself: An Epilogue*. New York: Norton.

Doolittle, H. (1956). *Tribute to Freud: With Unpublished Letters by Freud to the Author*. New York: Pantheon.

Dorsey, J. M. (1976). *An American Psychiatrist in Vienna, 1935–1937, and his Sigmund Freud*. Detroit, MI: Center for Health Education.

Dupont, J. (1988). Ferenczi's "madness". *Contemporary Psychoanalysis, 24*: 250–261.

Edmunds, L. (1988). His master's choice. *Johns Hopkins Magazine*, April: 40–49.

Ferenczi, S. (1932). *The Clinical Diary of Sándor Ferenczi*. M. Balint & N. Zarday Jackson (Trans.), J. Dupont (Ed.). Cambridge, MA: Harvard University Press, 1995.

Freud, S. (1904a). Freud's psycho-analytic procedure. *S. E.*, 7: 249–254. London: Hogarth.

Freud, S. (1905a). On psychotherapy. *S. E.*, 7: 257–268. London: Hogarth.

Freud, S. (1905e). Fragment of an analysis of a case of hysteria. *S. E.*, 7: 7–122. London: Hogarth.

Freud, S. (1911–1915). Papers on Technique. *S. E.*, 12: 85–156. London: Hogarth.

Freud, S. (1912e). Recommendations to physicians practising psycho-analysis. *S. E.*, 12: 111–120. London: Hogarth.

Freud, S. (1913c). On beginning the treatment (Further recommendations on the technique of psycho-analysis I). *S. E.*, 12: 123–144. London: Hogarth.

Freud, S. (1916–1917). *Introductory Lectures on Psycho-Analysis. S. E.*, 15–16. London: Hogarth.

Freud, S. (1926e). *The Question of Lay Analysis. S. E.*, 20: 183–250.

Freud, S. (1927a). Postscript to *The Question of Lay Analysis. S. E.*, 20: 251–258. London: Hogarth.

Freud, S. (1955a). Original record of the case of obsessional neurosis (the "Rat Man"). *S. E.*, 10: 259–318. London: Hogarth.

Freud, S. (1985). *The Complete Letters of Sigmund Freud to Wilhelm Fliess, 1887–1904*. J. Moussaieff Masson (Ed.). Cambridge, MA: Belknap.

Freud, S., & Abraham, K. (2002). *The Complete Correspondence of Sigmund Freud and Karl Abraham, 1907–1925*. E. Falzeder (Ed.). London: Karnac.

Freud, S., & Ferenczi, S. (1993). *The correspondence of Sigmund Freud and Sándor Ferenczi: Volume 1, 1908–1914*. E. Brabant, E. Falzeder, & P. Giampieri-Deutsch (Eds.). P. T. Hoffer (Trans.). Cambridge, MA: Belknap.

Freud, S., & Ferenczi, S. (1996). *The correspondence of Sigmund Freud and Sándor Ferenczi: Volume 2, 1914–1919*. E. Falzeder & E. Brabant (Eds.). P. T. Hoffer (Trans.). Cambridge, MA: Belknap.

Freud, S., & Ferenczi, S. (2000). *The correspondence of Sigmund Freud and Sándor Ferenczi: Volume 3, 1920–1933*. E. Falzeder & E. Brabant (Eds.). P. T. Hoffer (Trans.). Cambridge, MA: Belknap.

Freud, S., & Groddeck, G. (1974). *Briefe über das Es*. M. Honegger (Ed.). Munich: Kindler.

Freud, S., & Jung, C. G. (1974). *The Freud / Jung Letters*. W. McGuire (Ed.). R. F. C. Hull & R. Manheim (Trans.). Princeton, NJ: Princeton.

Freud, S., & Pfister, O. (1963). *Psychoanalysis and Faith: The Letters of Sigmund Freud and Oskar Pfister*. H. Meng & E. L. Freud (Eds.). New York: Basic.

Gardiner, M. (Ed.) (1971). *The Wolf Man*. New York: Basic.

Gay, P. (1988). *Freud: A Life for Our Time*. New York: Norton, 2006.

Grinker, R. R. Sr. (1975). Reminiscences of Dr. Roy Grinker. *Journal of the American Academy of Psychoanalysis, 3*: 211–221.

Grinker, R. R. Sr. (1979). *Fifty Years in Psychiatry: A Living History*. Springfield, IL: Charles C. Thomas.

Goldmann, S. (Ed.) (1985). Sigmund Freuds Briefe an seine Patientin Anna v. Vest: Eine Kur aus der Frühzeit der Psychoanalyse. *Jahrbuch der Psychoanalyse, 17*: 269–337.

Haynal, A. (2007). Freud psychothérapeute. Essai historique. *Psychothérapies, 27*: 239–242.

Haynal, André (2009). Notizen und Fragen an Freud und Frau G. zum "Fall G.". Ernst Falzeder (Transl.). In Anna Koellreuter (Ed.). *"Wie benimmt sich der Prof. Freud eigentlich?": Ein neu entdeckes Tagebuch von 1921 historisch und analytisch kommentiert*, pp. 237–245. Gießen: Psychosozial-Verlag.

Jones, E. (1955). *The Life and Work of Sigmund Freud (Volume 2)*. New York: Basic.

Kardiner, A. (1977). *My Analysis with Freud: Reminiscences*. New York: Norton.

Kriser, R. (1954). *Erinnerungen*. Unpublished manuscript. Library of Congress, Manuscript Division.

Leitner, M. (2001). *Ein gut gehütetes Geheimnis: Die Geschichte der psychoanalytischen Behandlungstechnik von den Anfängen in Wien bis zur Gründung der Berliner Poliklinik im Jahr 1920*. Gießen: Psychosozial.

Lévy-Freund, K. (1990). Dernières vacances des Freud avant la fin du monde. *Coq-Héron*, Nr. 177 (July): 39–44.

Lynn, D. B. (1997). Sigmund Freud's psychoanalysis of Albert Hirst. *Bulletin of the History of Medicine, 71*: 69–93.

Lynn, D. B., & Vaillant, G. E. (1998). Anonymity, neutrality, and confidentiality in the actual methods of Sigmund Freud: A review of 43 cases, 1907–1939. *American Journal of Psychiatry, 155*: 163–171.

May, U. (2006). Freud's patient calendars: 17 analysts in analysis with Freud (1910–1920). *Psychoanalysis & History*, 2007, *9*: 153–200.

May, U. (2007a). Neunzehn Patienten in Analyse bei Freud (1910–1920). Teil I: Zur Dauer von Freuds Analysen. *Psyche—Zeitschrift für Psychoanalyse, 61*: 590–625.

May, U. (2007b). Neunzehn Patienten in Analyse bei Freud (1910–1920). Teil II: Zur Frequenz von Freuds Analysen. *Psyche—Zeitschrift für Psychoanalyse, 61*(7): 686–709.

May, U. (2008). Nineteen patients in analysis with Freud (1910–1920). *American Imago, 65*(1): 41–105.

Obholzer, K. (1980). *Gespräche mit dem Wolfsmann: Eine Psychoanalyse und die Folgen*. Reinbek: Rowohlt.

Pohlen, M. (2006). *Freuds Analyse: Die Sitzungsprotokolle Ernst Blums*. Reinbek: Rowohlt.

Roazen, P. (1969). *Brother Animal: The Story of Freud and Tausk*. New York: Random.

Roazen, P. (1971). *Freud and His Followers*. New York: Alfred A. Knopf.

Roazen, P. (1992). Freud's patients: First-person accounts. In: T. Gelfand & J. Kerr (Eds.), *Freud and the History of Psychoanalysis* (pp. 289–306). Hillsdale, NJ: Analytic.

Roazen, P. (1995). *How Freud Worked: First-hand Accounts of Patients*. Northvale: Aronson.

Rudnytsky, P. L. (2002). *Reading Psychoanalysis: Freud, Rank, Ferenczi, Groddeck*. Ithaca, NY: Cornell.

Ruitenbeek, H. M. (Ed.) (1973). *Freud as We Knew Him*. Detroit, MI: Wayne State University Press.

Schur, M. (1966). *Das Es und die Regulationsprinzipien des psychischen Geschehens*. Frankfurt: Fischer, 1973.

Stern, A. (1922). Some personal psychoanalytical experiences with Prof. Freud. *New York State Journal of Medicine, 22*: 21–25.

Tanco-Duque, R. (1988). Bemerkungen zur Abstinenz in der analytischen Situation. In: *In Memoriam Igor A. Caruso* (pp. 77–84). Salzburg: Österreichische Studiengesellschaft für Kinderpsychoanalyse.

Tögel, C. (2009). Sigmund Freud's practice: Visits and consultations, psychoanalyses, remunerations. *Psychoanalytic Quarterly, 78*: 1033–1058.

Walter, B. (1946). *Themes and Variations*. New York: Knopf.

Weiss, E. (1991). *Sigmund Freud as a Consultant: Recollections of a Pioneer in Psychoanalysis*. New Brunswick, NJ: Transaction.
Winnicott, D. W. (1962). The aims of psychoanalytical treatment. In: *The Maturational Processes and the Facilitating Environment: Studies in the Theory of Emotional Development*. (pp. 166–170). London: Hogarth, 1965.
Wortis, J. (1984). *My Analysis with Freud*. Northvale: Aronson, 1994.

CHAPTER SIX

Notes and questions for Freud and Ms Guggenbühl talking about the "G case study"

André Haynal*

T he following text does not set out to prove or achieve anything. It does not present ideas that illustrate Ms Guggenbühl's discourse. I just want to follow this discourse like a *third ear;* I want, so to speak, to *rummage* in it for a little bit. After all, it invites us to look back and reflect on how a specific therapeutic concept and its underlying theory was put into practice at a specific historical point in time.

What we cannot see clearly here is the theory. Even though it happens before our very eyes, we cannot spot it. What we can make out are images of a life, and a will to live. We are looking at a new culture that the analysand represents, but which cannot come to light easily. In the background, we see a Freud who is addressing us as a teacher. We are met with memories that are, as memories tend to be, distorted and disfigured. Of course, memories are always more than the sum of single souvenirs, keepsakes, or mementos. However, the process of

---

*Translator's note: the English version of this article is based on the German version, which is itself a translation from the French by Ernst Falzeder (Notizen und Fragen an Freud und Frau G. Zum "Fall G." In: A. Koellreuter (Ed.), *Wie benimmt sich der Prof. Freud eigentlich? Ein neu entdecktes Tagebuch von 1921 historisch und analytisch kommentiert.* Gießen: Psychosozial-Verlag, 2009).

recalling—as this particular discourse seems to call out to the author of this chapter in the year 2008—can never completely free itself from the single instances of memory. Old pictures engage us when they show things that no longer exist: these records tell us *what exactly* was got rid of in acts of "chimney sweeping". Remembrance always amounts to more than memories and keepsakes, but these memories and keepsakes suggest in themselves that remembrance without them would not be possible. Old documents rouse our interest when they can show us something that no longer exists in this specific form, but the repercussions of which are still present, and can still be felt today.

A modern woman becomes a doctor and is determined to live an independent life. This woman remembers Freud, her *liberator*, in a piece of writing. In 1921, seven years after "Remembering, Repeating and Working-Through" (Freud, 1914g), Freud presents himself as the teacher of such a liberation. As he said about himself, "one works the best of one's power, as an elucidator (where ignorance has given rise to fear), as a *teacher*, as the representative of a freer or superior view of the world" (Freud, 1895d, p. 282, italics AH). Obviously, for the patient he embodies an authority, a teacher. Whether Freud still generally saw himself as such a teacher in 1921, or whether this was in fact peculiar to Anna Guggenbühl's treatment, can probably no longer be determined from the present viewpoint. Perhaps he approached this special case more as an analytic psychotherapy than as an actual analysis, that is, as a treatment focusing on *solving* a specific problem, which seems plausible also because of the therapy's short duration. The patient, and also her social environment, obviously saw Freud as The Great Man. In a letter of 17 June 1921, Guggenbühl's mother refers to Freud's work:

> I also wondered if Prof. Freud couldn't give you an hour a day during the holidays, too. Such an interruption is really not good; especially as he himself emphasises in his book that there is something like a Sunday hour, which has to be resolved on Monday. You could easily go to the same place where he spends his holidays, or what do you think about that? How long are Freud's holidays, anyway? Six weeks? Or longer? It's all so difficult. (cf. Koellreuter, 2007)

At the beginning, topics emerge that Freud seems to leap at immediately (fighting the younger brother, masturbation). On the other hand, they could be artefacts stemming from an unintended selection by the patient. In any case, we see that Freud quickly comes up with a courageous, even bold, reconstruction in which he prises apart three levels: the analysand's relation to the parents, that to the brother, and finally her conflict with Richard. All these elements are understood as constituents of an Oedipal conflict: the analysand wants to put herself in her mother's place after a maternal "breach of fidelity".

The script goes as follows: as noted before, a young woman does not want to do what she is told, but rather something that appears to be so much *freer* to her ... To submit to expectation, or to take one's freedom, that is the question; *to be free or not to be, that is the question*.[1] But is this permitted? The problem presents itself in the form of a doubt. And Freud understands it: he takes the side of freedom. From Freud, the young woman receives support *in accord with* her preconscious expectations: Freud turns into a friend.[2] She is encouraged to live the life she thinks she needs to live. The analysand seems to picture Freud as a teacher and a friend, as a friendly teacher with considerable authority.

This is the point where once again we need to stress the possible methodical constraints of the narrative. We may assume that the analysand only wrote down what *she herself* considered interesting or significant, which is why these notes necessarily represent a personal selection. According to the notes, and as already addressed above, Freud begins by tackling themes of the forbidden (pulling out a sapling on the balcony, pinching the little brother, masturbation). Is it Freud himself who accentuates these themes, or is this accent an artefact, a product of the "third ear" of the person who records the conversation?

After mentioning the various acts of "bullying", the analysand remembers scenes from her time in grammar school. She thought she "would like to love a youth who is immensely sad, and life would be made possible for him through me, and he would also be happy then" (no date, p. 3):[3] an interrelation between torment and redress that is reminiscent of Melanie Klein. In addition, she associates that she wants to have children. But the children are killed by the men, the *Hungerueli Isegrind* and the tomcats devour the children. What is surprising from today's point of view is that Freud—like in many other instances in this narrative—refrains from commenting here; at least according to this record. Perhaps he was not very talkative—as we know from other memoirs, he could be quite reserved. On the other hand, he could also indulge in long lectures. The report at hand includes examples of both attitudes.

When we look at all the themes that Freud picked up and interpreted during this treatment, we find those that concerned him all his life, that have turned into central hubs in his theory, and that build up around the Oedipus complex: *father, Oedipal jealousy, the wish to substitute the same-sex parent, fear of castration, bisexuality.*[4] After all, according to his own accounts, the woman's inner life, and the answer to the question "what does a woman want?" was more or less kept from him throughout his working life. The often-quoted *dark continent* (Freud, 1926e) and the fact that he frequently remarked upon woman's enigma—which, supposedly, "throughout history, people have knocked their heads against" (Freud, 1933a, p. 113)—did not seem to trouble him too much in this particular case; only sometimes are there echoes of jealousy and envy that resemble later Kleinian theory.

As de Saussure (1956) emphasises in an article on the occasion of his former analyst's 100th birthday, he had the impression that Freud, by the early 1920s, was more concerned with presenting and discussing his own ideas, than with discovering new angles in his patient's discourse. Formulating from today's point of view, Freud apparently continued an ongoing auto-analysis using the material brought in by his patients. One fundamental sensibility seemed to be that one understood in the other those things that one had discovered within oneself. This angle had already surfaced, though in a hidden form, during Freud's controversy with Fließ (1985). After all, Fließ expressed the opinion that Freud would uncover in his analysands' material what he, beforehand, had projected there himself. *According to Freud*, Fließ had *accused* him of something "which deprives my work of all its value: 'the reader of thoughts merely reads his own thoughts into other people'" (Freud, 1895d, p. 447). In a modern form, however, this could also mean that the analyst can only understand in the patient what has already become sufficiently clear and understandable in their own analysis within themselves (which is a strong argument for training analysis, and highlights the importance of countertransference!).

The thematic complex of *taking off*, of leaving a family that one (the analysand?) does not feel one belongs to, leads to an association with Schnitzler's romantic novella *The Shepherd's Pipe*. Perhaps the novella's young protagonist, who wants to leave her still new marriage behind and is encouraged to follow her longing desire by her husband

(Freud?), is a picture with almost prophetic qualities, in which Anna Guggenbühl's later decision can already be foreseen.

According to the records, we can see that Freud developed the analysis predominantly on the basis of *The Interpretation of Dreams* (Freud, 1900a). It is not transference but dreams that give this interaction its first meaning. Later on, however, it seems as if Freud grows tired of this predominance of dreams, and he comments that there are people who had "enough mental material at their disposal [to] solve everything within their psyche" (15 April, p. 11). Freud also assumes that the analysand's flight towards her father means that the father was her "first lover" (18 April, p. 16). Earlier, he had suggested the lovers as a substitute for the brothers (no date, p. 5), and had himself referred to his own publication about Dora (Freud, 1905e). Therefore, he puts Anna Guggenbühl in Dora's place—which probably is a distressing memory to him. Freud also assumes that the fact that Anna is very aware of her love for her brother "is useless, you cannot free yourself from it, because it has deeper roots" (18 April, p. 17).

The phrase "I was being dreamed" (19 April, p. 17)—which recurs at regular intervals, while other possible expressions like "I dreamed" are not used once—convey an atmosphere in which the analysand could inspect her *Id*, which needed interpretation, in her dreams. She also needs Freud in order for him to correct her. She draws closer to the idea "how it might be" to sleep with the father; however, she is quick to add, "just as a game, without desire" (19 April, p. 18). Thus for her it is not a wish, but an opportunity for thought, a "game". Or is her remark ("just as a game, without desire") a *negation or disavowal*? Does Freud comment aloud? Or does he keep his thoughts to himself? What thoughts exactly? Do they have anything to do with the crossed-out fragment "I am surprised, however, that ..." (19 April, p. 18) that follows? Most likely, we will never know.

Once again, the subject of separation comes into play, without being interpreted as such by Freud. In contrast, he speaks of the death of the mother "that is wished for" (19 April, p. 19)—also a separation! Anna Guggenbühl goes on to speak of the termination of various relationships; a possible prelude to her later decision to break her engagement?

When discussing a dream (21 April, p. 21) in which she helps "Oesch ... get over a wall" and then is "embraced", Freud surprises us with the following sentence: "Let us insert the symbols that we know thanks to our insights" (21 April, p. 22). So Freud apodictically posits the "insights" as shared. When the analysand relates a dream and her association about a chess board, and remembers that her father and mother used to play chess "before they became engaged" (21 April, p. 22), Freud intervenes: "You are free to insert the symbols yourself, so that you can make a connection *when you get stuck with the associations*" (21 April, p. 22f, italics AH). About the wall that needs to be overcome for the embrace, he comments: "It is the hymen." Here, the analysand's personal associations are being replaced by the method of "interpretations of symbols", like in the sections in *The Interpretation of Dreams* that were, under the influence of Stekel and others, added in later editions. Or does this impression rather arise from the selection made by the author of the notes, that is, by the analysand? It is possible that the interpretation of symbols impressed or affected her most, and gave her the impression that she finally *really* pushed towards *the id*. Or could this—very much to the contrary—also be an expression of her resistance, since the focus on the more general interpretation of symbols allows her to turn away from, and write less about, matters of a more personal nature?

In his interpretational work, Freud is strongly led by his own conceptions. For instance, there seems to be no doubt for him at all that "the sun always stands for the father" (21 April, p. 24). Then he insists that he himself represented *the father*, and that this fact provoked Anna Guggenbühl's resistance, like, for instance, the "idea that the cure is of no benefit" to her (22 April, p. 28).

At this point, beating fantasies are brought into play: "this means for the girl (child) to be loved in a sexual way" (22 April, p. 28). Freud shows a strong interest for this topic. Can we assume that he is influenced by his daughter Anna's analysis, which took place while he was treating Anna Guggenbühl (22 April, p. 27), and which he also dealt with in his publication "A Child is Being Beaten" (Freud, 1919e)?

Following this, Freud indulges in Viennese sarcasm: "Aha, a Swiss national diagnosis!" (22 April, p. 30), a remark followed in the analysand's notebook by *three empty pages*—a break of three days between 22 and 25 April. Could it be that she was offended?

Is it, then, some sort of compensation when Anna Guggenbühl continues her notes by thinking of the aged Goethe, and expresses the idea that she "might want to marry someone older" (25 April, p. 31)? Freud, of course, reads this idea as "transference to the father". This section is one of the few throughout the diary to explicitly address transference.

This is followed by close examination of the dynamic of *self-deprecation* the analysand displays. Freud interprets it by referring to examples of "other women" deprecating themselves, who "for instance [might] say they've got haemorrhoids"—a remark upon which, for Anna Guggenbühl "[n]othing comes to mind" (26 April, p. 35). To Freud, this is "a spec.[ial] resistance". Anna is taken aback: "I cannot tell you how much I like you; I think I've never loved anybody that way before" (26 April, p. 35). Unimpressed by this declaration of love, Freud knows better. Without flinching, he continues: "This love *for your father*" (26 April, p. 36; italics AH). Obediently, Anna resorts to associating about her childhood, which gives Freud the opportunity to address the lady with the *haemorrhoids* and Anna's self-deprecation once again, which, according to Freud, the analysand instrumentalises to disappoint him. We can see that *dealing with love* was not all that easy even for Freud.

Is it *half a slip* (if such a thing exists) to say that the father had "erot. [ic] feelings *against*[5] me" (26 April, p. 41), instead of *for* me? A *choice* of words; not necessarily a *mistake* in choosing words; but nevertheless an interesting twist that may insinuate that this love was probably also experienced as aggression.

In this context, nudity is brought into play: in the nude, she takes a walk with her father. Is this an erotic seduction, or at least an attempt at it? A sort of consolidation follows, a drop of blood on a finger (4 May, p. 2:2), gonococci (4 May, p. 2:1), all of which, in the interpretation, can be connected to genitalia. In further entries are condemnation, disfigurement, castration (no date, p. 2:16), and "*sale boche*"[6] (10 June, p. 2:17).

We can see how heavily Freud's interpretational work was influenced by his own conceptions and theories. What is astonishingly scarce is any discussion of the relational aspects, the play of transference and countertransference; in fact all affective dimensions in general, which barely seem to surface at all. We can see how Ferenczi and Rank were needed to point psychoanalysts towards the relational dimension, and let them become susceptible to it. After all, we do not know what Freud *sensed*. Still, this document shows that he did not give much account about it to others (and perhaps also to himself). From a wealth of examples, I could only discuss a few here, but nevertheless they show how psychoanalysis has developed and evolved continuously ever since.

In 1921, Freud was apparently holding on strong to many of his original ideas. For a long time, the image of a man "of noble simplicity and silent grandeur" (a famous expression of Johann Joachim Winkelmann, 1717–1768) was projected onto him; a man who proceeds incessantly, *without swerving* or aberrations. However, this image, drawn in the traditional literature, is corrected by Freud himself when he explores other parts in later stages of his work; for instance, in his observations on female sexuality, on fetishism, and, after 1936, on Moses and other topics. In 1921, however, it is still a long way to these sensibilities. It is understandable that Freud's contemporary Vienna circle upheld this image, and tried to preserve it when in emigration, especially in North America and in the Hampstead group in London. At the same time, it is also understandable that the more therapeutically inclined analysts like Ferenczi had to depart from this way in some aspects at least. And finally, what is also understandable is Ferenczi's concern about an increasingly dominant ego psychology (Ferenczi, 1932), which is about to take central stage. As a consequence, Ferenczi, Rank, Reik, Reich, Federn, and Weiss fall along the wayside, Helene Deutsch falls into line, and Abraham's Berlin becomes the leading model in Europe, and later also in the United States, in particular in New York. The politically savvy but always slightly paranoid Melanie Klein kept referring to Abraham, though she actually meant Ferenczi at least some of the time; she also slowly, unwillingly, and with considerable caution began to speak about countertransference in the analytic situation.

We get to feel that psychoanalysis is constantly *evolving*. The era of the *"primal analyses"* (Which was when? During the early analyses of hysteria? During the times of the Wolf Man and the Rat Man?) was over in 1921, but it is nevertheless still strongly *present*. Let us just think of how different this analysis is from others happening at the same time—for instance, by Ferenczi in 1921—or from analysis today, in this new millennium, in Paris or London, which will probably focus more on analysing relationships and affects. Do these differences exist because, as is often implied, Freud was primarily interested in theory, in *metapsychology* (anthropology), and thus understood his patients as material, a sort of fodder for this endeavour? Ferenczi writes about this in his 1932 diary, and quotes Freud referring to his patients as "rabble" and "only any good for making money out of, and for studying" (entry from 12 June, Ferenczi, 1932, p. 118). Without any doubt, however, and in spite of his fatigue and his limited therapeutic pursuit, Freud here showed a sincere *interest* in Ms Guggenbühl and provided his time and his energy cooperatively and empathically to her (and, we can assume, also to others). It seems incomprehensible that it is still possible for serious publications today to claim that psychoanalytic practices or techniques have not changed (Fonagy & Target, 2003).

The analysis at hand is a milestone in an era that would later be considered as classic. Studying it, we can discern and analyse this era's basic concepts and its limitations. When exploring Anna Guggenbühl's diary, readers may be inspired by their own fantasies; in any case, their exploration will be interesting and at times also pleasant and amusing.

Speaking from a historical perspective, I want to close with the following observations. All major themes of the *Freudian* fantasies are present. Nevertheless, Anna feels understood, and can finally make the desired, important, and (for her) probably also appropriate decisions. Digressing from its starting theme, the analysis moves towards questions that no longer quite correspond to the initial problem. To the contemporary reader, the records cast a flashlight on Freud's actual methods of treatment at the time, albeit perhaps refracted by Anna Guggenbühl's personal selection, which probably only includes what she found most important. We can only wonder why the play of transference and countertransference, and of affective exchange, which is vital to present-day analytic ideas, is obviously absent. *Tempora mutantur nos et mutamur in illis.*[7]

Notes

1. Translator's note: phrase in italics is English in the original.
2. Translator's note: the name "Freud" and the German word for friend, "Freund", are very similar. AH highlights this similarity with italics in his original German text: "Freud verwandelt sich in einen Freund" (Haynal, 2009, p. 236).
3. Unless otherwise noted, dates and page numbers correspond to dating and pagination in the diary.
4. Words in italics are in English in the original.
5. See corresponding translator's note in the diary.
6. Means in a French vulgar language: "dirty German". (It can also been applied to another German speaker.)
7. Times change, and we change with them.

References

Ferenczi, S. (1932). *The Clinical Diary of Sándor Ferenczi*. M. Balint & N. Zarday Jackson (Trans.). J. Dupont (Ed.). Cambridge, MA: Harvard University Press, 1995.

Fliess, W., & Freud, S. (1985). *The Complete Letters of Sigmund Freud to Wilhelm Fliess 1887–1904*. Cambridge, MA: Harvard.

Fonagy, P., & Target, M. (2003). *Psychoanalytic Theories. Perspectives from Developmental Psychopathology*. London: Whurr.

Freud, S. (1895d). *Studies on Hysteria. S. E., 2*. London: Hogarth.

Freud, S. (1900a). *The Interpretation of Dreams. S. E., 4–5*. London: Hogarth.

Freud, S. (1905e). Fragment of an Analysis of a Case of Hysteria. *S. E., 7*: 7–122. London: Hogarth.

Freud, S. (1914g). Remembering, Repeating and Working-Through (Further Recommendations on the Technique of Psycho-Analysis, II). *S. E., 12*: 147–156. London: Hogarth.

Freud, S. (1919e). A Child is Being Beaten. *S. E., 17*: 179–204. London: Hogarth.

Freud, S. (1926e). *The Question of Lay Analysis. S. E., 20*: 179. London: Hogarth.

Freud, S. (1933a). *New Introductory Lectures on Psycho-Analysis. S. E., 22*: 5–182. London: Hogarth.

Koellreuter, A. (2007). Als Patientin bei Freud 1921. Aus dem Tagebuch einer Analysandin. *Werkblatt: Zeitschrift für Psychoanalyse und Gesellschaftskritik, 58*: 3–23.

de Saussure, R. (1956). *Sigmund Freud*. In: H. M. Ruitenbeek (Ed.), *Freud as We Knew Him* (pp. 357–359). Detroit: Wayne State, 1973.

INDEX